Clericalism
Stories From The Pews

If the Catholic Church is to continue to grow into the church that God wants it to be, it will need to deal with clericalism. The change will need to be structural and related to the way power is shared among the People of God. Gideon Goosen provides a roadmap through some difficult terrain, wrestling with obstacles such as an infantilised laity, to a productive place where all the People of God are recognised for their baptismal dignity and equality. Some will need assistance to recognise and grapple with the way language, including theological language, honorific titles, and "man-made misogyny" contribute to a church community struggling to attain its full potential. This book provides stories from people in the pews which are instantly recognisable, along with historical and theological insights and spiritual encouragement advantageous for the journey.

Patricia Madigan O.P.
Centre for Interfaith Ministry, Education and Research
(CIMER), Sydney.

Goosen's book brings to mind a comment by an Irish bishop: 'Ordaining a woman is anontological impossibility'. He offers us a theology at ground level, based on examples and personal experiences of clericalism in the life of the Church. He is searching for ways to change the clerical culture which Pope Francis has identified as a major problem. It is based on binary thinking: the laity are the not-clergy, men take precedence over women, priests are not so much pastors as managers who assume their parish is 'theirs' to control. Seminary training produces an attitude of entitlement and superiority. Co-responsibility, notinfantilising the laity, is called for, and Goosen provides frequent discussion questions which will make readers think through the issues. He concludes with practical steps towards gradually eliminating clericalism from church life. On the eve of the Plenary Council of theAustralian Church his book could not be more timely.

John D'Arcy May, Irish School of Ecumenics,
Trinity College Dublin.

Gideon Goosen's fine and clear discussion of the often dysfunctional attitudes of clergy to laity in the Catholic Church deserves wide reading. He outlines the history and prevalence of clericalism and invites his readers to imagine and push for more mature relationships.

Andrew Hamilton S.J.
Editorial consultant of Eureka Street;
policy officer with Jesuit Social Services

Through personal story, Scripture and theological reflection, this highly accessible, engaging and everyday workbook for parishes invites Catholics, in particular, to consider the current culture of our church and offers practical possibilities for shared conversation and action on ecclesial transformation.

We are reminded that our attitudes and behaviour convey our values to one another and to the world. In this time of Plenary Council dialogue, discernment and gathering on listening to what the Spirit is saying, *Clericalism: Stories From The Pews* is vital reading for all parish communities. Designed as a workbook, with excellent questions for conversation, it sheds light in uncomfortable corners of our church that we may not have recognised or been able to name, but almost certainly have experienced, or even practised. The illumination is stark: clericalism is a way of being that denies dignity to self and to others; clericalism touches many lives, whether part of the Catholic community or beyond; clericalism is not part of the Gospels and has no place in church and no place in society.

Whether you seek to effect change or to remain as is, the daily question for every Catholic is how to be faithful to the way of Christ in all we are and in all we do. The format and the content of this workbook is a contribution to assisting us all, in every arena of church, to listen deeply to what the Spirit is saying and to discover ways of acting more authentically and with greater integrity in every aspect in the life of our church.

Geraldine Hawkes
Formerly, General Secretary of the South Australian Council of Churches (2007-2019)
Inaugural Chair, Commission for Australian Catholic Women (2000-2006)

'Clericalism: Stories From The Pews' is about a central roadblock to the renewal of the Catholic Church. Although antithetical to the teachings of Jesus, clericalism is shamefully the prevailing culture in the Church. Gideon Goosen discusses clericalist behaviour by clerics – often reinforced by lay people – that prejudices the practice of Christianity and the efficacy of the Catholic Church. This is a workbook with valuable case studies and provocative questions that initiate discussions on the nature of this blight and ways of eradicating it. More importantly, this is about all the Catholic faithful – both clerics and lay people – being treated and behaving as baptised adults, all responsible for their Church and its Christ-centredness. Goosen also draws attention to the misogyny in the Church which is a key aspect of clericalism. This book should be invaluable to those Catholics who recognise the importance of understanding all the manifestations of clericalism in order to ensure its eradication, and to get our Church back on mission.

Peter Johnstone MA (Theol)
Member and former president of Catholics for Renewal;
Convener of the Australian Catholic Coalition
for Church Reform

Clericalism: Stories From The Pews A Workbook for Parishes is a timely and valuable resource that can take forward the work of the Australian 2021 Plenary Council. It explores convincingly the nature of clericalism as an 'illness', lethal for the life of the Church. The 'workbook' makes use of real life narratives and the methods of listening, dialogue and discernment. The tone is urgent, but the writing is expressed without rancour. Firmly grounded in Catholic theology and history, this is an authoritative call to action for the elimination of what Pope Francis terms 'an ugly perversion'.

Trish Hindmarsh
Formerly, Director of Catholic Education Tasmania.
Active member of Concerned Catholics Tasmania
and Women and the Australian Church (WATAC).

STORIES
FROM THE PEWS

A WORKBOOK FOR
PARISHES

Clericalism

GIDEON GOOSEN

COVENTRY
PRESS

Published in Australia by
Coventry Press
33 Scoresby Road
Bayswater Vic. 3153
Australia

ISBN 9780648725190

Copyright © Gideon Goosen 2020

All rights reserved. Other than for the purposes and subject to the conditions prescribed under the *Copyright Act*, no part of this publication may be reproduced, stored in a retrieval system, or transmitted in any form or by any means, electronic, mechanical, photocopying, recording or otherwise, without the prior permission of the publisher.

Scripture quotations are from *The Jerusalem Bible* © 1966 by Darton Longman & Todd Ltd and Doubleday and Company Ltd.

Cataloguing-in-Publication entry is available from the National Library of Australia http://catalogue.nla.gov.au/.

Cartoons by Graham English

Cover design by Ian James - www.jgd.com.au
Text design by Megan Low (Film Shot Graphics FSG)
Set in Noto Serif

Printed in Australia

Contents

Abbreviations 11

Dedication 12

Acknowledgments 12

Introduction 13
The culture of clericalism – The meaning of clerical – Aim of this book

Case 1 Bishops and breastfeeding 24
The power of the clergy - How could clericalism have been avoided here? - Conscience - Sources of clericalism

Case 2 Our church or your church? 39
Alternative responses – The bishop who spent too much – Ownership – Reclaiming the church – Models of church - What is clericalism? - Definition - Homosexuality and secrecy - Clericalism is contagious - Mind your language - Unexamined assumptions - Other opinions on clericalism – Pope Benedict on clericalism – Seminary system: think again - Preparation of future pastors – Learn with whom?

Case 3 Abuse of power 74
Valuing people - 'Father-knows-best' syndrome —Priests are not supermen or the "ontological change" problem - Criticism of "ontological change" - The servant model is the antidote - The importance of synodality

Case 4 Infantilising the laity............... 99
Lay people can be guilty of clericalism – The principle of subsidiarity – Pope Francis on Infantilisation – The bureaucrat's prayer – Co-responsibility – The desire to clericalise everyone – The strength of Baptism and the role of the laity – Positive Inclusive vision – The divine energy- Integrated approach – Examining the documents – Definition of laity - Dualism – Inclusive spirituality – Clericalism and role of priests – Laity as priest, prophet and king

Case 5 Mad-made misogyny 128
Rejection and discrimination – Misogyny: some history – Women and Vatican II - Women priests? – Mary Magdalene.

Do something near you.................... 142
Progress slow: four warnings – Conclusions – Do something - Structural and governance changes – Educational and attitudinal changes

**Appendix: A gospel roadmap
to avoid clericalism** 164

Abbreviations

AA	*Apostolicam Actuositatem* (The Decree on the Apostolate of the Laity)
ACBC	Australian Catholic Bishops Conference
CCC	Catechism of Catholic Church
CEO	Chief Executive Officer
CL	*Christifideles Laici* (On the Vocation and the Mission of the Lay Faithful in the Church and In the World)
CNR	Catholic National Register
ESCT	European Society of Catholic Theologians
GS	*Gaudium et Spes* (The Pastoral Constitution of the Church in the Modern World)
LG	*Lumen Gentium* (the Dogmatic Constitution of the Church)
NCR	National Catholic Reporter
PDV	*Pastores Dabo Vobis* (Post-Synodal Exhortation, Pope John Paul II)

Dedication

This book is dedicated to those courageous people, women and men, who came forward to tell their personal story about clericalism in the church in the hope that the church will grow into a more mature community where people are equal in their discipleship of Jesus Christ.

Acknowledgments

Let me thank all those involved with the creation of this book: Hugh McGinlay, the ever-helpful editor and publisher; Graham English, whose cartoons help us to see the funny side of serious issues; those who contributed to this book through their often painful stories; those who wrote generous endorsements of the book; my colleagues, friends and family whose encouragement supported the whole project; and Margaret Knowlden whose writings about clericalism inspired the idea of writing a book which deals with a topic others would rather avoid.

Introduction

In his engaging book, *The Shanghai Free Taxi*,[1] the journalist, Frank Langfitt, describes the situation of society in modern China with regard to the Communist Party. Their unchallenged rule allows them to do what they wish, like taking land from farmers to build factories, throwing people in jail without trial or banning Google. The government has all the power, the middleclass and peasants have none. Langfitt describes poor farmers, "the simplest in the world", with very low demands. After decades of poverty and isolation, they are happy for any scraps the government tosses their way. When the government does a bit for them, they feel it is a huge blessing. Grovel, grovel.

Those in the Communist Party, and the very rich, feel they are meant to rule and exercise power while the peasants expect nothing and are grateful for any crumbs that fall off the table.

This situation is not uncommon in a variety of countries and institutions. One group of people leads a privileged life, rules over the rest, and are not accountable to others, be they government or institutions. The "rest" accept their fate and have few, and very modest, expectations.

In the Catholic Church (and other churches), this can be called clericalism. One group (the clergy) have all the

---

[1] Frank Langfitt, *The Shanghai Free Taxi*, London: Weiden & Nicholson, 2019.

power, rule and are not accountable to the rest. The rest simply accept that is the way things are and have few and very modest expectations. As children sometimes say, "You get what you get, and don't get upset". The origins of the word "clergy" and its history will be pursued shortly.

Vatican II (1962-5) has changed all that, at least theoretically, pointing out that all Christians are equal through their baptism. All the baptised constitute the church. The church is now a community of equals, or a community of disciples of Jesus. Although there is still a hierarchy, decisions should be made after discussion, listening to others and consensus. It is the synodal system. It all sounds very idealistic.

We come across clericalism, in the sense of some being superior to others, in many hierarchies. The police force, the army, banks, governments, corporations, netball associations, hospitals, even Vinnies, Anglicare, the Salvation Army or Unitingcare. All of these have a pecking order and people have their place in that order. Although these may have some great and idealistic ideas about all being equal in the association, in reality, the hierarchical nature comes to the fore with power and privilege being concentrated in the hands of a few. It is all about an institutional elite seeking to maintain power in a group. That is human nature you could argue. It occurs in all human institutions including the church. We should not be afraid to confront the element that is human in the church.

On the other hand, we don't want to come across as too worldly and lacking in piety if we always raise issues of human weakness in the church. Archbishops do not like to be reminded that they are weak humans. We prefer to speak of the "holy" church rather than the "church" with many

Introduction

human weaknesses. The frequent use of the expression "Holy Mother Church..." always seems to me as a frantic and pious attempt to forestall or anticipate any contradictory voice. Who would dare to challenge a teaching from "Holy Mother Church"? Well, it turns out that "Holy" Mother the Church is not always so holy.

Christians have often been conned by being told we are a spiritual group and should listen to the clergy. A discussion of power and abuse of power is not becoming for a Christian church! This argument can be a very astute and successful tool in the hands of the men (and in the Catholic church it is only men) who enjoy a privileged life, to manipulate the masses and maintain the status quo.

Let me say at the outset that this book is not a campaign to get rid of priests. That would miss the point entirely and be quite a wrong interpretation of the aim of this book. The anticlerical republicans during the late 19th century had as their mantra "Clericalism is the enemy!" That is not what I am promoting. This book does not try to put clerics against the laity. We are one church. We, clerics and lay, are against the clericalism of which we are all guilty to a greater or lesser degree. (Because clericalism is so important, it is one of the most frequently addressed topics of Pope Francis' talks and homilies. We will be continuously referring to his thoughts on the matter.)

The Christian community will always need an ordained pastor who will celebrate the Eucharist with the community, celebrate the other sacraments, and evangelise. This book is not anti the clergy. This book is aimed at how we can recognise patterns of behaviour which we call "clericalism" and which are plaguing all in the church, ordained and lay, men and women, young and old. As Andy McAlpin, a

Dominican priest, points out: "Clerics are not the only ones who are clerical. College professors, bosses, lay ministers, journalists, politicians, etc., can all lay claim to clericalism, which finds its roots in false or misused authority by the clerical class. This is a most unfortunate reality, as the clerics claim to know and fully understand God's word and desire for human flourishing. Clerics have dropped the ball on this time and again".[2]

The culture of clericalism

This brings us to the idea of the "culture of clericalism". By the culture of an organisation we mean the way that institution functions, the pattern of behaviour that characterises the institution. The banks in Australia have been through a royal commission and are trying to change their culture. It has been a culture of maximising profits and neglecting people. The system of giving bonuses to staff who perform well for the bank has led to some staff being unjust to customers and gaining personal financial gain in doing that. In the insurance branch of one particular bank, for example, the staff realised that they could maximise profit by rejecting many justifiable claims while selling as many insurance policies (and sometimes unwanted) as possible. This culture places profit above persons. That was the culture that permeated the banks. Now, after the royal commission, the problem is to change that culture. Where do you start?

We can take another aspect of a culture, the use of water. What is our water culture? With frequent droughts and with climate change, the importance of changing our culture towards water will have to change. One could say that we in

---

[2] Andy McAlpin, "Pope Francis and Clericalism", *NCR*, December 17, 2013.

rich western countries are very wasteful of water. Drinking water is flushed down the toilet, taps are left running, rain water is not harvested, crops that require too much water are chosen, half-full dishwashers are turned on, grey water is not re-cycled, showers are too long. There are many ways we could be less wasteful. This requires a change of culture regarding water. We could refuse to change, but then we, and our children and grandchildren, would have to bear the consequences.

Another useful word here is that of "enculturation". When a child grows up in a certain environment, it becomes enculturated into that culture. It absorbs the values and behaviours of that culture without any reflection. This happens only once in our lifetime. The reflection on values and behaviours might come later in life and the culture can be modified. So it is with religion which is a part of a larger concept called culture. A child is born into a religious culture and grows up with those values and behaviours.

The culture of the church is the way members go about doing things in the church, the values and attitudes they adopt. These include priorities like buildings, maintenance, fundraising, caring for people, good liturgies, good preaching, and the way parishioners relate to one another and to the pastor and the way the pastor and the parish committees relate to parishioners. That culture has been driven by clericalism (a concept we will examine in more detail in Case 2 below and throughout the book). Historically, we now have the problem of how we get rid of it (or the bad elements in it), or how we can change that culture.

The meaning of clerical

It is important to recall that the meaning of the word "clerical" changed over time. Originally, it did not apply only to priests.

In fact, the Greek word *kleros* (from which "clergy" came) had nothing to do with religion. It meant, a "lot, an allotment, a piece of land, an estate, a heritage". What was inherited, the thing shared, was quite mundane and secular: physical property. Then it came to be a sociological term that names the fact that society recognises a certain segment of its members as having recognisable social features and norms that distinguish them from the rest of society. People with certain gifts in society began to be recognised for these gifts and treated differently. They were grouped together and given a name, physicians, teachers, lawyers, soldiers, ministers.

This secular meaning was gradually transformed by the Christian community to mean persons functioning within the priesthood of all people but ordained. Once these people were grouped together and formed the "clergy", the idea of the laity (those who were not ordained) was also formed. Clericalism was, in a way, something that evolved with time, or as Susan Reynolds, an assistant professor of Catholic Studies at Emory University, points out: "Clericalism – the elevation of ordained persons over the laity – is not only an unintended consequence of history, but also a social sin, an idolisation of power perpetuated by a constellation of social structures and cultural practices."[3] Today Catalysts for Renewal make a simple statement about this separation and appeal to the Gospel. They say: "Clericalism causes a

---

[3] Susan Bigelow Reynolds, "Everybody Wants a Revolution, but Nobody Wants to Do the Dishes" *CNR* 23 May 2019.

Introduction

'them and us' mentality, a separation between clergy and people. We would like to see our bishops and pastors follow the example of Jesus and his explicit directive to the apostles: 'If anyone wants to be first, he must make himself last of all and servant to all' (Mark 9:35). In their leadership positions, bishops need to be accountable to the People of God".[4]

Then, much later, the word "clerical" took on the meaning of "office work" which one parishioner offered as a meaning when I ask him what "clericalism" meant. So we must be alert to different meanings of the word "cleric" and "clerical".

Let me go back to groups of professionals forming "clerical" groups. This has some very good outcomes in terms of addressing problems and issues that are common in that profession. It provides support to fellow "clerics" (read "colleagues"), it can be a way of sharing knowledge and providing help in difficult situations. It can help to promote research in that profession and establish codes of conduct.

However, the coming together of clerics can also have negative outcomes. The group can think it is superior to other groups. Lawyers or politicians may think they are above the law, for example, or doctors might think they control life. It can lead to usurping power in a society, in influencing politicians, in bullying or manipulating people, in sexually assaulting people and thinking you can get away with it. These are all bad outcomes, and we are familiar with these in contemporary society.

Today "clerical" and "clericalism" is most often used in association with priests or ministers of religion. It is usually

---

[4] Catalysts for Renewal, submission to the Plenary Council 2020, "The Future of the Catholic Church in Australia". February 2019. http://catalystforrenewal.org.au

interpreted as having negative overtones. When the church is accused of "clericalism", no one is paying the church a compliment.

When priests form a clerical group they can also have positive outcomes such as sharing effective pastoral approaches, improving preaching, doing in-servicing together, improving liturgies, learning conflict management skills, etc. However, that aspect has been comprehensively overshadowed by recent scandals, in particular the worldwide child sexual abuse scandal and the misuse of money, both of which are connected to clericalism in the negative sense.

Aim of this book

The focus of this book is on the negative aspects of clericalism because the alarm bells have gone off and the lights are flashing. Clericalism has been identified as a big contributing factor to the church's current ills. Pope Benedict XVI and Pope Francis have made this abundantly clear although some bishops are still in denial. Other bishops have joined in the appeal for change. For example, many German bishops, according to the ESCT Newsletter, demand changes concerning the structure of the church, "since the abuse that has happened is considered to be an abuse of power rooted in clericalism, the dominance of male persons, and sexual immaturity. For instance the Bishops Wilmer of Hildesheim, Feige of Magdeburg, Bätzig of Limburg, Kohlgraf of Mainz, and Bode of Osnabrück, demand serious changes to access to the priesthood, division of power, and limitation of power".[5]

At the more local level, *Concerned Catholics* at a well-attended meeting in Canberra in 2017 put it bluntly: "This was a night

---
5   European Society of Catholic Theologians, *Newsletter, 42nd* 11 March 2019.

for the laity. And what the speakers delivered was a message that contemporary clericalism must change or the church faces a lingering malaise of decline and irrelevance".[6]

The aim of this book is, therefore, to analyse what clericalism is through the experience of others and the words of leaders, and to suggest ways of overcoming it. The point of departure is not some textbook theories about clericalism but the real life stories of people in the pews. You can contradict a theory but you cannot gainsay someone's experience.

The importance of analysing clerical culture is emphasised by Clete Kiley who once served as executive director of the committee on priestly life of the U.S. Conference of Catholic Bishops and as principal staff person in the late 1990s on what was then the ad hoc committee on sexual abuse, and who got to the heart of what's missing in the ongoing discussion of abuse. "I'm going to keep returning to this idea of (clerical) culture", he said, "because we haven't unpacked that enough. We've changed policies and procedures and, to some degree, they've been effective. But we did not really analyse culture."[7]

Offering an amendment to the proposed standards of accountability for bishops, Bishop Steven Biegler of Cheyenne, Wyoming, outlined several "values for episcopal conduct". He wrote in part:

> As the Church seeks to be reformed, we need to address the root causes of the episcopal abuse of power in the sexual abuse crisis. A major factor was clericalism. Some bishops fostered a "toxic brotherhood" which caused them to overlook questionable behaviour,

---
6 Mark Metherell, "The Need for Catholic Church Reform", *Concerned Catholics*, 15 May, 2017.
7 *NCR*, 16 November 2018.

ignore rumours of problems, believe clerical denials and seek to preserve a cleric's ability to minister. At times, they acted to protect the reputation of the Church or clergy, while they shunned the victims/survivors of sexual abuse and their families. Bishops frequently ignored the voices of the laity who spoke up about sexual abuse and the mishandling of allegations; instead, they acted within institutional isolation.[8]

This book relies heavily on the living experience of people in the church. As we listen to them, we can piece together the many elements that go into the clerical culture. We can also ask ourselves how clericalism in these cases could have been avoided. It is up to everyone in the church to make an effort in trying to rid the church of clericalism. Why do we have to eradicate clericalism? Because it tears the church apart. It leads to rejection and discrimination, to feelings of not being listened to, to feelings of being second class members of a church. It also led to the scandalous incidents of child sexual abuse in the church, shameless cover-ups and in some cases to outrageous misuse of church money.

The frequent discussion questions YOU SPEAK, WE LISTEN are essential to the book which aims at getting parishioners involved in talking about these issues and working out ways at overcoming clericalism. The assumption is that the church is ours – all are stakeholders in carrying out its mission.

The names of the participants, whose stories we will hear, and other details, have been changed or omitted as the aim is to discuss the relevant issues, not the individuals. Actual names occur only where the stories have been

---

[8] Brian Roewe, "Bishops anticipating action on abuse, settle for a metaphor", *NCR*, 14 November 2018.

published elsewhere. There is no bibliography at the end of the book, as the sources are mentioned in the footnotes as we go along. Many of these footnotes refer to current articles on the topic of clericalism.

The case studies, the stories of contributors, which are like chapters in a book, will introduce us to various aspects of clericalism. However, the discussion and questions will roam over many topics more or less connected to clericalism. Here and there, it will be necessary to probe deeper into some issue from a historical or theological viewpoint, to throw light on an important dimension of clericalism. It is not necessary to read the case studies in chronological order although Case 2 includes a good broad discussion of clericalism.

The last "chapter" is meant to encourage parishioners to be active, to do something – however great or small – to eradicate clericalism.

Case 1

Bishops and breastfeeding

We will come to the detailed definition of clericalism below in a future chapter. For the moment, we have said clericalism is about some in the church feeling superior to others. We will expand on this in due course. Rather than talk endlessly about "clericalism", let us start by listening to someone who has endured clericalism.

We start by listening to Margaret who has experience of pre- and post- Vatican II days. This story refers to a time before Vatican II when Catholics had to abstain from food and drink twelve hours before receiving Communion. It has since been repealed. Margaret gave us the following extraordinary story from her own experience.

> The law of fasting from midnight before receiving Communion was also set in stone. So when my mother, nursing her tenth child, asked the Parish Priest if she could have a glass of water after midnight, he didn't know the answer but referred it to the bishop who

(hardly an expert on breast-feeding) replied 'No'. Today it beggars belief that she even thought it necessary to ask the question.

This a good example that raises a few issues for reflection. Although Margaret is shocked that her mother should even think of asking permission to have a glass of water before Communion, it does show us very clearly how much the clerical ethos had penetrated the church. The first thing that strikes us is the assumption by the bishop that he knew something about breastfeeding. He assumed his authority applied in areas when he had no experience. Far from not being an expert, he would have been ignorant of what breastfeeding is about. This attitude is a mark of clericalism.

Before analysing the above story further, let me give you another example from someone's experience. It is Raimondo, in his seventies, who is a regular attender. It stresses the attitude that father can do everything and make all decisions without outside help.

> In a new parish many years ago, but in the post Vatican II era, I was keen to see if I could join the liturgy committee. I was sent to a certain lay person's home to enquire. When I finally found the person concerned and asked if there was a liturgy committee, he said 'No there is not. If there are any decisions to be made, father makes them'.

You Speak, We Listen

Q: If you have doubts about what action to take, to whom do you go for advice? And why that person?

The power of the clergy

The clerical ethos or attitude in the church did not happen overnight. It has evolved over centuries. The Christian churches of the first century, after the death of Jesus Christ, were small communities of believers in a world of "other religions" like the Mystery Religions of Rome and elsewhere. In his letters, Paul mentions the different gifts in the church– the teachers, administrators, healers, preachers, miracle workers, prophets, those who speak in tongues and those who interpret them, but no mention of the person who prayed the Eucharistic Prayer (called the *anaphora*) and presided over the Eucharist.

The church was a group of believers with different gifts used for the community. In the catacombs the Christian community would have assembled around a table structure in one of the alcoves, surrounded by the graves of diseased brothers and sisters. Someone in the group who have been designate to lead the Eucharistic prayer even before the prolific writer and theologian, Hippolytus of Rome, had (allegedly) written his prayer that later became so famous and well used in the Latin Rite.[9] That person, the presider, was one of the group. In the catacombs of Priscilla, (named after a wealthy Roman woman who owned the property and led the community), who knows who she would have got to lead the prayer? Perhaps another woman of faith. The point is that whoever led the prayer was just one of the group, not someone who thought they were superior to the others in the group.

It was only later, and especially in the fourth century, after Constantine, that a group of people arose who formed a

---

9 This version of the anaphora was called the *Anaphora of the Apostolic Tradition*.

caste of "priests" and were paid for by the state. They became more and more distinct from the other Christians and hung onto clothing that soon distinguished them from others. Thus two groups arose: the clergy and the laity. With that, the attitude of clericalism (feeling superior to others) grew and settled into the church and became part of the church culture. Already the culture of all being equal was changed to a superior group and the lesser members. This is a good example of how the culture of a group can change. Christians born (or converted into Christianity) after this change would have been born into a culture of clericalism.

During the Dark Ages, monks and monasteries played a big role in preserving the church heritage but bishops continued to rise in status as they acquired wealth, property and influence. This reached great heights in the Middle Ages when bishops were more like lords, or princes and the Pope like a monarch. Europe had no countries as we have today. The church provided some structure and rules for living, and grew in influence as most of Europe converted to Christianity. People were largely uneducated,(the image of the great warrior, Charlemagne, taking out his slate at night in his tent in Aachen and practising the letters of the alphabet comes to mind),especially before the discovery of the printing press, but the clergy (some of them) had some education so could easily lord it over the peasants.

The power of the clergy over ordinary people was maintained by firm teachings, excommunication, and threats of eternal damnation if doctrines were not followed; and sometimes even physical torture. Belief and superstition were often intermixed as people struggled to make sense of life and death, goodness and evil, misfortune, disease and healings, and natural disasters. Women who had knowledge of herbs and healings were called witches and were judged as evil as the men in charge could not handle their strange knowledge. All this helped with the construction of the pedestal on which the clergy were placed as they were thought to have all the answers.

Now consider the two stories above. In Margaret's story, the bishop thought he could make a judgment on anything because he was a bishop. After all, he had the centuries-old heritage of bishops behaving in that way.

In the second story, by not seeking outside help and making all the decisions, the priest indicates that he sees himself as the law maker in that community, the privileged one who knows better than anyone else. This question of knowing better than anyone else is important in this context for a number of reasons. The training of those to be ordained cannot cover all fields of knowledge. While future pastors concentrate on theology, their contemporaries at university are studying business, finance, psychology, science, I.T. communications, etc. These people are better prepared in many areas of knowledge that the pastor. He should stick to what he knows and listen to others on topics about which he knows little (like breastfeeding!).

Clericalism can also be seen in the women's ordination debate. Pope John Paul II tried to close down debate by ordering people not to talk about it. Others, near to the Pope, have said statements by the Pope on the issue were infallible. This is an example of thought-control, a characteristic of clericalism. The bishop in our story above made a decision without consultation on a topic about which he knew little. On women's ordination, surely an open discussion throughout the world, with discernment and prayer, is the life-giving approach. The Holy Spirit should not be shut out in an attitude of clericalism, but invited in.

How could clericalism have been avoided here?

To return to our story: Margaret's mother could have acted differently. The point about her mother asking such a question is important here because she (unreflectively and unknowingly) is endorsing the clericalism that the story reveals. But we all do it. We have got used to asking the parish priest all kinds of questions that we could decide for ourselves according to our conscience. However, by asking these questions we assist in maintaining clericalism in the church.

We can work towards eliminating clericalism by *not* asking those questions. Margaret's mother could have reasoned with herself that the area of breastfeeding is beyond the expertise of the bishop and that she could make up her own mind. However, at this time in the life of the Catholicism (prior to Vatican II), people were not encouraged to think for themselves.

What about the bishop? He seems to be a good example of clericalism which Andy McAlpin defines as "simply the disordered idea that by virtue of one's office, all proclamations made by the perceived or actual authority must be followed regardless of contrary evidence or differing opinions".[10] The bishop is saying "Do as I say because I am bishop". On the other hand, the bishop could have avoided clericalism also by responding to Margaret's mother by admitting that this topic was beyond his expertise and by encouraging independent thinking and decision-making on the part of Margaret. The

---

10   McAlpin, op.cit.

decision could have been left to her conscience, but in those days the church preferred to tell people what to do rather than to help develop their conscience. Even after Vatican II, some bishops were inclined to not respect the decision of Vatican II that each person should follow their own conscience. Added to this was the obligation to inform and develop one's own conscience.

(Going back to the 1960s, prior to Vatican II, a Dutch bishop I knew once pointed out how selective lay people could be about asking the clergy questions. He said that many people would ask all sorts of moral questions about sexual matters and contraceptives, but no one ever asked him if selling their second-hand car for a certain price was morally okay! So there were some areas where lay people *did* feel they could decide what is right and what is wrong!) One can

understand the hesitancy of some bishops who did not like the idea of following one's own conscience – this could lead to individuals making their own decisions and thus escaping the control of the clergy. A strong element in clericalism is the desire to control the laity because the clergy know best.

In Raimondo's story, the lay person that Raimondo spoke to had absorbed the clerical attitude very well when he said that father will make any decisions that need to be made.

Let us go to politics to give a parallel example. It is well known that Australia has many droughts and bushfires. In 2019, the Co-ordinator for Drought in Australia wrote in his report to the Prime Minister the following:

> As a consequence of climate change, drought is likely to be more regular, longer in duration, and broader in area. It means that farmers and communities who rarely see droughts are likely to see it more often. And those that have been managing drought for many years may now see it intensify beyond their lived experience. Ultimately, the nation could see some areas of Australia become more marginal and unproductive.[11]

The Prime Minister refused to meet with the Co-ordinator of Drought and also a group of former Fire Chiefs. Here is another example of the person in charge (PM) knowing best and making decisions (including taking no action) without consulting experts first. This is neglect of taking steps to be informed on an issue by those who know. One can only conjecture as to the motivation behind this lack of action. One possibility is that taking action might provoke a political reaction from the climate deniers in and out of

---

11 Paul Bongiorno, "A Burning Issue", *The Saturday Paper*, 16-22 November 2019, p. 15.

the Government. So ultimate political self-preservation, and hanging onto power comes first. Bishop Bransfield's story in the next chapter will show how donating huge sums of money to fellow bishops could also be seen as an attempt of self-preservation in church politics. This is a bit like the Lukan account of the steward who quickly bought off his master's debtors so that, when he was fired, he would have friends.

We can conclude that Margaret's bishop, Raimondo's parish priest and the Australian PM all seem to think that they can make decisions relying on their power rather than informed consultation.

Conscience

The above stories about Margaret and Raimondo touch on one's attitude towards conscience. Neither person was expected to follow their conscience, they were to follow the decisions made by authority, that is, the bishop or priest. Vatican II had something to say about that. It changed the way Catholics should balance conscience and authority, making one's own conscience supreme.

One can find a beautiful paragraph on conscience in the Vatican II document *Gaudium et Spes*, 16. The lead up to conscience is well expressed in the context of God wishing everyone to be saved. It is worth pondering these insights because they paint the big picture. Paragraph 16 is talking about the People of God and how they relate to God. It also talks about those who have not heard the gospel. The plan of salvation also includes those who acknowledge God as Creator. These include Moslems who adore the One and Merciful God. God as Saviour wishes *everyone* (it says "men" but means everyone!) to be saved.

Then there are those who, through no fault of their own, do not know the gospels, yet moved by God's grace, try by their actions, to do his will *as it is known through their consciences*. Included too are those who have not yet arrived at an explicit acknowledgment of God, yet strive to live a good life. And what is this thing called "conscience"? The document says conscience is something in which everyone detects a law which they do not impose upon themselves, but which holds them to obedience. Conscience calls everyone to do good and avoid evil; this is God's law tattooed on everyone's heart. In obeying this law, people manifest their human dignity, and avoid blind choices. This conscience is the "most secret core and sanctuary" of people in which they are alone with God and can hear God's voice in the depth of their being.

Then another document of immense significance for the church, *Dignitatis Humanae*, emphasises freedom of conscience. I will cite the relevant sentence but avoid the sexist language: "It follows people must not be forced to act contrary to their conscience. Nor must they be prevented from acting according to their conscience, especially in religious matters" (#3).

In applying conscience to an issue, Frank Brennan provides six useful steps: examination of the presenting problem; exploration (probing for clarity); evaluation (of all the elements that go into the decision); ethical stance (the norms and regulations we find necessary), ethical action (going ahead with the action), and re-evaluation.[12]

The bishop assumed he had the knowledge to make a

---

12 Frank Brennan, *Acting on Conscience*, St Lucia: Queensland University Press, 2007, cited in Berise Heasly, *Call No One Father*, Bayswater: Coventry Press, 2019, 128. For further reading on conscience, see Linda Hogan, *Confronting the Truth: Conscience in the Catholic tradition*, Mahwah: Paulist Press, 2000.

decision on breastfeeding. The office of being a bishop would cover him in all situations. That is the essence of clericalism. As Andy McAlpin said above: clerics claim to know and fully understand God's word.

As we listen to stories from a variety of people, we will come across issues which collectively combine to give us what we call clericalism.

You Speak, We Listen

Q: Can you name incidents when you have experienced clericalism in the church?

Tell the group about these.

Q: What changes in the behaviour of those people in your stories would have to change to avoid clericalism?

Q: In your experience, do people still ask too many questions of their pastors rather than consult their own conscience?

Does the age of the person (their generation) make a difference?

Q: How were you taught to think about conscience? How would you explain the difference between conscience and "blind choice"?

Sources of clericalism

The topic of clericalism is being explored in these pages and it is hoped by the time we come to the end with all our stories, a good general idea of clericalism will be evident. In Case 2 we will analyse some definitions of clericalism, but for the moment let us consider some of the sources of clericalism.

Our guide will be an excellent discussion of clericalism by a retired pastor in Washington, Peter Daly.[13] He traces the origins of clericalism. He maintains that clericalism comes from four sources which feed into what becomes the attitude of clericalism. Here is a diagram which illustrates this.

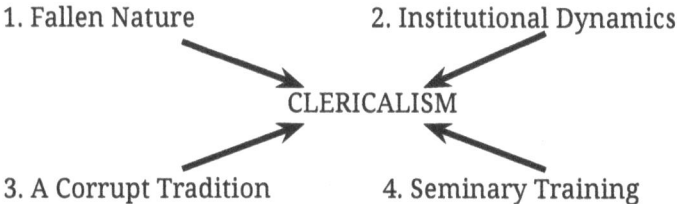

1. Fallen Nature   2. Institutional Dynamics
                CLERICALISM
3. A Corrupt Tradition   4. Seminary Training

First, "fallen nature" (Daly's term. We might prefer, "flawed nature" or "human imperfection"). By fallen nature is meant the way we are which is prone to sin. We have a built-in weakness to do the wrong thing. At the centre of this is our pride as the Garden of Eve myth teaches us. The seven deadly sins sum it up pretty concisely: pride, anger, lust, envy, gluttony, avarice, and sloth. (Daly suggests the mnemonic PALE GAS will help us recall the seven.) Given that we all suffer from our fallen nature it is logical that people will never overcome their attitude of superiority and elitism entirely. We will never overcome this weakness entirely. No perfect world here.

Secondly, institutional dynamics. Institutions work in a certain way. They are hierarchical and if you want to get to the top you have to work to that end. This applies to all kinds of groups of people – corporations, the military, politics, universities or the police, as well as the church.

Those who see their priesthood as a career rather

---

13 Peter Daly, "Clericalism", *National Catholic Reporter*, 19 February 2019, accessed 31 October 2019.

than a service ministry will do what it takes to further their ambitions. That means getting close to those in power and pleasing them. Daly refers to them as "climbers", "kiss-asses", "suck-ups" and "kick-downs". There will always be these people in any organisation but in the church we can change the criteria of those who get promoted. Change the dynamics and we change the outcomes.

Pope Francis has already started this process of change, by changing the criteria of those he chooses as cardinals and bishops. He chooses those with great pastoral records and who have embraced the poor and are involved in social justice issues and interfaith dialogue. The criteria of a PhD in Canon law is no longer a priority.

Daly suggests that no one should be made a bishop unless they have spent at least ten years in a parish as a parish pastor. The old route of ordination-bishop's secretary-auxiliary bishop-bishop-archbishop-cardinal should be totally rejected because of the lack of pastoral work in a parish.

Let me give an example of the above. Giovanni Montini, later Pope Paul VI, for example, is the quintessential case of what has happened in the past. He was born in Brescia in 1897. He was educated by the Jesuits, and then in 1916, at the age of 19 years, entered the seminary. He was ordained in 1920 and studied Canon Law and then studied at the Gregorian University and La Sapienza University - both in Rome. He was then invited into the Secretariat of State in the Vatican which marked the beginning of his career as a diplomat. He was never appointed parish priest anywhere or any time.

The point is that parish pastoral work should make the average person empathetic to others. To understand daily living, to "smell the sheep" as Pope Francis says, one needs to spend time with them. (Note the number of bishops/archbishops in the sexual abuse cases who could not show any empathy for the victims.)

Thirdly, a corrupt tradition. We know that Jesus in the gospels taught his disciples to be servants of others, never to seek the highest place at the table and to be self-sacrificing. Over the centuries, the church, being human, developed many aberrations that were not true and faithful to the gospels. Hence the recurrent theme of reform. Church leaders sometimes became powerful princes or lords or wealthy land owners and walked away from the gospel principles. Many reforms were necessary over the centuries and, as we all know, the church has to be perpetually reforming itself. One thinks of The Cluny reforms under Pope Gregory VII in the eleventh century (independence of the clergy, simony, lay investiture), the First Lateran Council (1123, celibacy for priests), the Fourth Lateran Council, Trent (1545, training for priesthood, doctrines against Protestantism), Vatican II (1962-65, liturgy, revelation, ecumenism, church, interfaith dialogue), Religious orders like the Franciscans, Dominicans, Benedictines, Cistercians, all have had their attempts at reform. No one is perfect.

Given that in recent centuries many bishops and church leaders have placed huge emphasis on their status (living in "palaces") on being superior to others (having undergone an 'ontological change'), on their wealth, or on their authority and power, it is not surprising that these distortions of the tradition have reinforced clerical attitudes.

Fourthly, seminary training. The seminary training of the past decades has been a contributing source of clericalism, some would say it has been the breeding ground for clericalism. Young men without much life experience are thrown together in a hothouse and told they are special and will receive special treatment and when their courses are completed they will "have" their parish. Everything is laid on for them. Courses with small numbers, accommodation and meals and daily Mass. Their diocese pays for their tuition. Nuns used to look after their domestic needs and meals, hence reinforcing misogyny. They have no financial worries. No women were allowed in the seminary except the nuns who were effectively servants. They lived a privileged life. In this a-typical environment they were supposed to learn the skills and knowledge of how to be a successful priest.

Daly certainly has honed in on a big issue. Who could blame seminarians for thinking they were special? Who could blame them if they left with an attitude of superiority and privilege? The secrecy was something they learnt from the culture within which they lived, and a sense of status was obvious from the way others deferred to them and the way they behaved.

If we take these four factors together we see what a powerful influence they collectively had in forming the clerical mind. It is our task to reverse these attitudes.

You Speak, We Listen

Q: *Considering the four elements above identified as the origin of clericalism, with which do you agree or disagree?*

Case 2

Our church or your church?

Having heard about bishops who want to be able to answer all questions, even those relating to breastfeeding, we can now examine some other angles on clericalism. Some parishioners feel like second class citizens because their opinion and work in the church does not seem to be valued. They feel like an outsider in their own church. One may ask: is it their own church? The stories below tackle this issue.

This incident was written by an experienced educator, Jocasta:

One of my Church History students at an academic institution told me that as a teacher in a local school, she was asked to do the reading at a school Mass. She made sure she wore her best slacks and jacket. When the Mass was over, the parish priest came to her and bellowed. 'Don't you dare read in my Church with slacks on'. Her reply was what he needed to hear but probably thought she was just a teacher being rude.

'Sorry, Father, I thought this was OUR Church!

Here again we have some important issues that jump out at us. The main point is the use of "my" or "our" and its implications.

We could be quite profound and theologically correct to say that the church belongs to Christ. It does not belong to the Pope or any archbishop, bishop or priest. Again, the first communities of Christians were followers of Christ. They came together on the Lord's Day to hear the Scriptures and celebrate the Eucharist. The group had the mission of spreading the good news. There were people with different gifts who had different roles in the community but no-one OWNED the church.

In this story, the pastor needs to remind himself that he was only a servant of the community not a dictator. If the issue was really about what to wear when attending the Eucharist, then the pastor could have put it on the agenda of the parish council (or liturgy committee) and have a civil discussion of appropriate dress in the context of that community, in that culture, and at that time in history.

In medieval times, in some small villages in Europe, the local parish priest might well have been the only person who could read and write. He might well have been the only educated person in the village so all people came to him for information and advice. Unfortunately, this only helped to cultivate the image of the omniscient priest on a pedestal which doesn't help us today.

It brings to mind another priest who when he first arrived in the new parish (I nearly wrote "in *his* new parish"!) assured the congregation that it was "your" parish not his.

But it soon became apparent when he personally chose the parish council members and others, that this was indeed *HIS* parish not *YOURS*.

Alternative responses

Perhaps here the young lady could have expanded on her reply to the parish priest. She could have explained her feelings of being made to feel that that the church belonged to the parish priest and how bad that rejection made her feel. She could have expanded and said how much time and effort she had put into the parish, into the liturgy over many years. She could also have pointed out that parish priests come and go; and to have someone act as if he owned the church treated her as insignificant.

He too could have reacted differently. He could have said to her, "Thank you for the reading today. I appreciate your contribution to the life of the parish. You and I must have a conversation with the liturgy committee at another suitable time".

The fact that the priest claimed it was his church is a recurrent theme in church history. Today's church is no better. We can learn a lot from the following sad story which made many Catholics very angry. As far as extraordinary cases go, the case of Bishop Michael Bransfield in the USA touches the extremes in terms of a most dramatic example. He thought that not only was the church buildings his own but all the revenue it earned as well.

The bishop who spent too much

Michael Bransfield was the bishop of the diocese of Wheeling-Charleston (Virginia) in the USA. His diocese was unusual regarding finances. The diocese had access to enormous wealth because of oil field royalties – which reportedly generated up to $15 million annually. In addition, the diocese had investment income on an endowment of $230 million – exceptionally rare for a diocese with fewer than 80,000 parishioners.

The scandal revolved around the extremely lavish lifestyle that Bishop Bransfield led. The facts are astounding. He spent nearly one million dollars on private jets and over $660,000 on airfare and hotels during his thirteen years as bishop of his former diocese of Wheeling-Charleston. Further details emerged that during his last year in active ministry, Bransfield took at least nineteen trips in what was described as a chartered luxury jet. Those trips cost the diocese more than $142,000.[14] It has also been reported that he gave money – US$29,000, that was not his to give – to the newly appointed Cardinal Kevin Farrell, prefect of the dicastery for Laity, Family and Life. The money came from church funds, in this case, a hospital.[15]

Flynn continues his report:

> Bransfield also spent thousands of dollars on jewellery and other clothing, including spending more than $60,000 of diocesan money at a boutique jeweller in Washington, DC during his time in office. The Diocese

---
14 J. D. Flynn, "Bishop Bransfield's Life of luxury", *Catholic News Agency*, accessed 14 November 2019.
15 Christopher Altieri, "New twist in Bransfield scandal comes amid Vatican financial woes *"Catholic Herald*, 27th October 2019, accessed on 14 November 2019.

of Wheeling-Charleston met the costs for Bransfield's travels to visit his family, and much of his month-long stays on the Jersey Shore. The diocese paid for a $276 purchase at a liquor store, as well as a month-long car rental for $2,975.

Bransfield submitted his resignation as bishop of Wheeling-Charleston when he turned 75 years. This was immediately accepted by Pope Francis. Following his resignation, Pope Francis ordered Archbishop William Lori of Baltimore to conduct an investigation into allegations that Bransfield had sexually harassed adult males and misused diocesan finances during his time in West Virginia.

What a woeful and scandalous story! However it highlights the issue, as does Jocasta's story, of who owns the church. This bishop thought that in being made a bishop all the money in the diocese was his personally. He thought it was his church. His habit of giving money to fellow bishops and archbishops was done to curry favour with them and possibly promotion when the opportunity arose. There have been other cases in Europe, for example, where the local bishop has spent millions of dollars on his "palace" with renovations and extensions. The Pope has had to step in and stop the waste of money which belongs to all in the church.

The difference between being the custodian of money and owning it personally has escaped some bishops and priests. It is also a good argument for limiting the power of bishops and priests. Referring to Bishop Bransfield, one can ask the question, "How does this happen without some kind of checks and balances?" "How did the Bishop get away with this for thirteen years?" There is definitely a lack of oversight in the church's present structures. This could be avoided by placing all money matters in the hands of a diocesan finance committee who can veto the bishop's request for money. The committee could be made up of lay and ordained, men and women. There has got to be better and safer ways of ensuring accountability. The days of a monarchical bishop are over. The powers of a bishop and parish priest have to be curtailed. The spending of parish priests also need some kind of monitoring. Some dioceses may well have a code of conduct on what the parish pays for and what the individual priest pays for, but to my knowledge this is never enforced or audited or even discussed.

The other issue here is a lavish lifestyle. The gospels point in the opposite direction for those engaged in ministry. They point to a lifestyle of simplicity, sharing and making do with the minimum.

Ownership

This attitude of entitlement and privilege – hallmarks of clericalism – is something some priests acquire in the seminary. In the following story, narrated by Raimondo, it is clear that some priests do see their appointment as parish priest as the occasion of their entry into *their* parish.

> Many years ago, a certain parish priest was appointed to our parish. I remember it well. On a Sunday morning, at the time of the homily, the new pp proclaimed how excited he was to have "his" parish and how pleased his mother was that at last he had been given "his" parish. He could hardly contain himself for joy. He then informed us that he would be taking his three weeks holiday in the snowfields immediately, but

would catch up with us on his return. Those in the congregation who could not afford a holiday in the snow were left to ponder their misfortune. This is a good example of entitlements.

The idea of ownership of anything related to the church needs to be re-visited. Church buildings and halls, to whom do they belong? Legally, it has to be the collective church, but when it comes down to the use of the church hall, for example, who decides? There needs to be some kind of delegated responsibility here. People, the parishioners who raised the money will feel that it is the local community's hall, not the parish priest's. Raimondo can relate an experience he had concerning this point.

> I recall asking a parish priest for permission to use the parish hall for a meeting of a reform group. He agreed quickly and then said, "Can you put that in writing?". I did this by email and then got a reply saying he had considered the request but he could not agree to it. I

wrote back asking for the reason for the refusal. The parish priest replied saying he would not enter into any discussion of his decision. I regard this as clericalism and an example of a lack of transparency. We should know the reason for the refusal. Who after all paid for the hall in the first place? The parishioners, and it was parishioners who wanted to use it.

On reflection, lay people should not have to ask permission for the use of their hall if the Building and Maintenance Committee is looking after the bricks and mortar. The parish council should be capable of drawing up guidelines for the use of the hall and then someone put in charge of adhering to those guidelines. If parish priests have all the keys, then they can control who uses the hall. Different to this case, there have been other instances when the local bishop can try to use his power to control who is allowed to make speeches or give lectures in his diocese by forbidding them use of church property. I think this is an atrocious abuse of power although renewal groups are quick to find another venue, sometimes belonging to another Christian church with more understanding and less clericalism!

Another incident which illustrates this control urge and rejection of open discourse which Pope Francis wants, is that of the Archbishop of Hobart, in July 2018, refusing to allow Frank Brennan to speak about same-sex marriages in Hobart, Tasmania.

What goes for church halls also applies to church buildings. The story is told of the brick basilica in Bologna, San Petronio, which was built by the locals in the fifteenth century. When the pope at that time visited the city, he tried to enter the basilica and claim it, but was told it was their cathedral not his! Among Orthodox churches, I have noted from time to time they have arguments about who owns the church. The laity have the keys and refuse to hand them over to a priest. In the final analysis everyone should feel it is theirs together and this feeling will help in the process of the laity assuming co-responsibility for the mission of the church.

Reclaiming the church

The case studies above raise the question of whose church is it? The meaning of "church" in this context might be ambiguous. It can mean both the physical building and the community of people, the parishioners with their pastor. Regarding the physical buildings, the Christian church was doing just fine until the Constantinian era when they moved from house churches to using the large basilicas in Rome and other buildings. These large basilicas were court houses in their time and were easily converted into churches. The shape of the buildings also meant people were further away from the altar or table compared to the intimacy of house churches.

This physical separation of the clergy from the laity became a metaphor for what was happening on the spiritual level. Unfortunately, acquiring physical buildings also meant more clergy were busy with buildings rather than people. It marked the beginning of amassing enormous real estate and a pre-occupation with bricks and mortar rather with pastoral issues. John Thornhill, a noted Australian theologian, remarked with a sense of cynicism, that whenever the Australian church had a serious pastoral problem it resorted to building something! I think there is a true saying that applies to the Catholic Church worldwide, notwithstanding all the enormous good work it does. The saying is this: "Money will possess you sooner than you possess it".

Regarding churches in both senses of the word, we can say it belongs to both clergy and lay people. But if lay people are to reclaim their part in it, they need to do something dramatic because in reality, the structures of the church are not inclusive. Bishop Ricardo Centellas of Potosi, in Bolivia, has a novel idea.[16] He suggests a woman be appointed the chair of the parish council and that she has the power to make casting votes and that the parish pastor does not have any veto rights. Imagine that! Of course, she would have to be progressive in her thinking and not a clone of previous pre-Vatican II parish priests. The agenda of council meetings would be so different.

Bishop Centellas went on to say something on churches and reform. He was responding to the idea springing from the Synod of Bishops for the Amazon (2019), that women should be made deacons and suitable married men be ordained. That would not change anything he said, because the "model of the church, which is too hierarchal, must change." No one is rejecting hierarchy as such but the Catholic Church has suffered from too much hierarchy. The model must change. This has already been alluded to by those women (and men) who do not want to be ordained into the current model of priest. If the model changes they would re-consider.

By model of church we mean a way of explaining what the church is and how it operates. Take a simple model : that of a triangle. The pope is at the apex of the triangle. Next down are the bishops who carry out his commends. Then come priests who carry out the commands of their bishops.

---

16 Junno Arocho Esteves, "Before new ministries, Church must eradicate clericalism, bishop says" NCR, 24 October 2019.

As the triangle gets bigger, we have lay men and lastly lay women who carry out the instructions of the priest. Their job is to pray, pay and obey.

This model is about hierarchy and the chain of command in the church. It is rather like an army. It tells you nothing about spirituality, or mission of the church. So it has its limitations. This was the popular model in recent centuries. Its advantage was that it was clear as to lines of authority but only saw the church from one angle, that is, from a hierarchical perspective.

No model is perfect. All have their limitations but to habitually use only one model is being myopic in terms of trying to understand the church. The church is multi-facetted. One model cannot tell the full story.

Models of Church

Triangle   Circle   Inverted Triangle   Polyhedron

  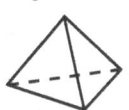

You Speak, We Listen

Q: *Try to explain to others around you what these models of church mean. Which do you think is a suitable model for today?*

Q: *Should a parish pastor discuss with parishioners before he is appointed to a parish what his idea of church is? What are the advantages and disadvantages of this?*

Q: *In Jocasta's story what was the pp's idea of church? What model of church did he seem to have?*

What is clericalism?

As we are going to reflect on clericalism in this book it is time to further investigate the meaning of the word. We have already given some idea what is meant by the word clericalism by Margaret's story and comments made above. Now is the time to pursue this further. If you ask people around you what "clericalism" is, you may get some strange answers.

I decided to use a dipstick approach and ask a few people. Here is what I got. I asked an elderly lady, sixty plus years and a regular attender, if she had heard of "clericalism" or what it meant. She looked me in the eye, puzzled and trying hard to come up with something. "No", she said, never heard of it. A second lady, about fifty, also a regular church goer, studied my face carefully and then said, "No" she didn't know the word. She knew "clerical" which she said had something to do with office work. I then added that "clericalism" had something to do with the church and attitudes involving the clergy. This immediately struck a chord within her. Her eyes lit up. Yes, she knew about the old ways of treating people and how heavy-handed priests and bishops could be. But not today (!). Then there was a young mother, late twenties, at the Eucharist celebration with her daughter who attended a class on First Communion preparation before Mass. When I asked her what "clericalism" was, she dismissed the notion immediately, saying she had never heard of it!

So there might be a problem with the word rather than the concept. People might not know the word but many have experienced clericalism. A young male aged twenty, a regular attender, said it meant nothing to him off the top of his head. Then a male senior server, aged 18, said he had no idea, but asked if it was related to "clergy". I said yes. Then when I asked if it had a positive or negative meaning for him, he immediately responded "positive". So much for adult education in the faith!

The response from the Plenary Council consultation in Australia was very different. It appears many people had indeed thought about clericalism. Here, in part, is what the report says about the meaning of clericalism:

> The theme most widely discussed by participants within the topic of Leadership and Church Governance was that of clericalism and the need to end it. The word "clericalism", although used often, meant different things to different people. For many, clericalism was "the boys club mentality" or "cronyism" or, as one participant put it, "a deviant culture of social elitism, entitlement and privilege which developed out of a particular theological understanding that, at ordination, a man's very being is elevated to a level of existence superior to that of other human beings."[17]

One last thought for this section is the question of all the assumptions that go into clericalism. George Wilson has pointed this out very strikingly. Behind every act, or thought, of clericalism is an assumption that we do not reflect upon. Wilson calls these unexamined assumptions.

You Speak, We Listen

Q: *What do you understand by the word "clericalism"?*

---

17 ACBC, "Listen to what the Spirit is Saying", *Final Report for the Plenary Council* Phase 1 : Listening and Dialogue. July 2019, 80.

Some years ago now, there was the high-up cleric who worked with the Bishops Conference. He said he did not know what "clericalism" was. I thought he might be joking. So I said I would send him the titles of some books to read, particularly George Wilson's book, *Clericalism: the Death of Priesthood*. So I did. Some months later, after the Christmas break, I spoke to him again, only to hear that he had not bothered following it up! That reaction says a lot. To me it indicated the arrogance of someone who does not want to learn or be taught anything.

This unwillingness to learn is surely a main element in clericalism. If I know everything, why would I bother with investigating something further. It also relates to another phenomenon I have noticed: the lack of in-servicing among the ordained. This is outrageous given that in today's world, pilots have to keep up their flying hours, teachers have to do in-servicing of the latest educational insights, doctors need to know the latest research into diseases and treatments, people doing I.T. have to keep up to date with cyber security in a rapidly changing technology. All this, and priests are not obliged to keep up to date with theology, liturgical reforms and pastoral work? I think the Catholic Church is paying the price for this neglect right now.

Some years ago, when working on a Diocesan Ministry Committee, we were discussing the options for in-servicing for priests. The bishop at the time said that a number of days were offered but the clergy were not obliged to attend. I thought to myself, "That is odd". The very people that need the in-servicing do not attend and those that do attend would probably update themselves anyway by way of reading or discussion.

This lack of in-servicing played out after Vatican II when many priests did not devote any time to learning about Vatican II and the new directions it was taking with regard to liturgy, new concepts of church as *The people of God*, ecumenism, and attitudes to faiths other than Christian. As the sociologist and Columban priest, Cyril Hally, used to explain it: On Saturday mornings, courses on Vatican II used to be offered. The priests were too busy in their parishes to attend; the religious brothers were out coaching their football teams, so the only ones to attend were the nuns. As a result, the female religious are the front runners in Vatican II theology.

A second, very serious aspect of the above is that many parishes did not have a dynamic *Continuing Adult Faith Development Program*. The parish priest was too busy, had too many things to attend to, had no ability (or feared) to delegate. This overreach only promoted clericalism. In some instances, good programs have been stopped. This has meant that many parishioners have been deprived of what should have been a great opportunity for growth in their faith. If the clergy were not up to date with Vatican II, how could one expect the parishioners to be?

Definition

If we look to a definition of clericalism, we can do no better than use the one George Wilson suggests in his book on clericalism.[18] Here is the gist of his definition:

> Clericalism is an attitude that grows out of a sense of privilege and superiority, secrecy and preoccupation with status among the clergy. It is an attitude that can apply to both clergy and laity.

---

18 George Wilson, *Clericalism: The Death of Priesthood*, Minnesota: The Liturgical Press, 2008.

We notice that it is an attitude and that lay people and as well as the ordained can have this attitude. It grows out a sense of privilege and superiority and we may well ask what are the origins of this sense of privilege? Secrecy is also a component part and we have comes across this many times in the church, not least in the sexual abuse scandals. Secrecy also quickly leads to outright lying. A preoccupation with status is also one of those things that is obvious to all except the person concerned. Clericalism is bad for priests because it distorts their mission and is harmful for the laity because it hinders their development as adult Christians. But let us first trace the origins of clericalism.

If clericalism were a disease, it might well be described in medical terms we all understand. (See *The disease known as clericalism* in the later section 'Clericalism is contagious' for a humourous example.)

Clericalism has indeed been described as a disease. Let me refer to Bishop Centellas again. When asked to elaborate on the role of women in the church, Centellas told CNS that currently the church is suffering from a serious sickness "that we have been fighting against for the past fifty years but have been unable to eradicate".

"That sickness is clericalism", he said. "So, it isn't a question of a diaconate for women or *viri probati*. The problem is the model of the church. I believe Pope Francis had a special intuition in his document *Episcopalis Communio* when he said that we must invert (the structure); lay people above, clergy below.»[19]

Pope Benedict XVI was struck by the disease of clericalism he saw in Cuba and Mexico on his travels. He spoke

---

[19] Esteves, op. cit.

of the political corruption and power abuse of the clergy and the neglect of faith formation of the (passive) laity.[20]

The negative pastoral consequences of this kind of clericalism are now stunningly clear. Facing the twin onslaughts of secularism in some circles and Pentecostalism pretty much everywhere, the Catholic Church across Latin America sustained massive losses in percentage terms during the late 20th century.

The church projects an image of power and privilege as we read above. Here is an example of just one of the privileges of a cardinal:

> Cardinals have in canon law a «privilege of forum» (i.e. exemption from being judged by ecclesiastical tribunals of ordinary rank): only the pope is competent to judge them in matters subject to ecclesiastical jurisdiction (cases that refer to matters that are spiritual or linked with the spiritual, or with regard to infringement of ecclesiastical laws and whatever contains an element of sin, where culpability must be determined and the appropriate ecclesiastical penalty imposed). The pope either decides the case himself or delegates the decision to a tribunal, usually one of the tribunals or congregations of the Roman Curia. Without such delegation, no ecclesiastical court, even the Roman Rota, is competent to judge a canon law case against a cardinal.(Canon Law #1405)

---

[20] John Allen, "Benedict's gentle debunk of clericalism", *NCR*, 12 March 2012.

Homosexuality and secrecy

Part of the above definition of clericalism is that it is "a sense of privilege and superiority, secrecy and preoccupation with status among the clergy". This points to the connection between the sexual abuse scandal and homosexuality in the church and clericalism. There has been a massive cloud of secrecy about these aspects which have finally come to view in all their ugliness. First of all homosexuality. There are a huge number of homosexual priests, bishops and cardinals in the church. Pope Benedict was shocked when he found out, after receiving a report which he ordered. The French journalist Frederic Mattel, among others, has exposed all of this in his book, *In The Closet of the Vatican*. [21]

The problem is that the church's teachings on homosexuality are at odds with the reality. The church has never come to grips with recent decades of scientific research into homosexuality and the human person which has brought us new understandings of this phenomenon. It has also not come to grips with the huge number of homosexual priest in its ranks. The result is that all homosexual priests have had to live with the tension of supporting the teaching of the church on homosexuality which says that homosexuality is an "intrinsic disorder" while they cannot accept it. "Coming out" was never an option. They were caught in a trap of dishonesty. Instead of the church being the safe haven for homosexuals, it has proved to be their nightmare. One cannot imagine the tension, stress and suffering in the lives of many homosexual priests over many years. The secrecy about all this meant a practice of "Don't ask, don't tell". The hierarchs in Rome were

---

21 Frederic Martel, In The Closet of the Vatican : Power, Homosexuality, Hypocrisy, London: Bloomsbury, 2019.

guilty of ingrained hypocrisy. Here was clericalism at work. There was a bond of secrecy about what was going on.

So too the secrecy came into play when there was child sexual abuse. It was known or suspected but the rule of secrecy made sure that the information did not get out.

Clericalism is contagious

The laity play this game and perpetuate the clericalism. Chloe gives us a good example of this complicity when she reports:

> Many others within our parish community have told me that 'Father should be asked' before I and other team members introduce any simple changes or additions. Even though the team in question has the knowledge, experience and should have the authority to do so.

This is important to acknowledge. It is easy to keep the focus on the ordained, but the laity are also implicated. Think of it for a moment. There would be no clericalism if the laity refused to go along with it. By remaining silent they went along with it. Me, you, just about everybody. The huge silence about it is another sign that in the past the laity accepted the passive role of the laity and a very high theology of priesthood.

The disease known as clericalism

Name: "Clericalism" or the "Yes-Father" syndrome.

Symptoms and signs: Diagnosis is normally straightforward. There is a tendency to elevate the ordained and adopt a submissive attitude in presence of same. A tendency to actually like being belittled and infantilised by the clergy. Often seen in people exaggerating the power and influence of the ordained.

Regarding the signs, a physical examination normally reveals very little although the clicking of heels is sometimes a telling sign or downcast eyes in the presence of a priest or bishop. Another sign is a sharp pain in the head whenever the words "democracy", "accountability", "gospel freedom", "feminism", "women priests" come into the conversation.

Occurrence: Seldom found in children under the age of fourteen, but affects males and females. Thought to be particularly prevalent among Roman Catholic, Orthodox and Fundamentalist Christians.

Severity: It may well be life-threatening among any group of Christians and is able to quash the Spirit and the life out of any community in no time. Light attacks of clericalism are seldom found as it normally exists in severe forms.

Treatment: Treatment is possible with varying degrees of success. Usually treatment starts with high doses of taking a deep breath and repeating to oneself that "the-ordained-are-not-supermen". Further treatment may include *logotherapy* regarding the meaning of words such as: *Father, superior, equality, baptism, transparency, infantilisation,* and cognate ideas.

For particularly severe cases, where no other treatment is successful, the severing of the ecclesiastical umbilical cord is advised. This procedure is available for out-patients and usually leads to a quick recovery, however a warning that this disease may re-occur even in elderly persons without any apparent reason.

In all cases, it is best to consult your trusted spiritual adviser or simply read the gospels.

Mind your language

The antidote to this attitude is to refuse to be complicit and to call out clericalism when we see it. Think of the contemporary feminist movement. The leaders in this movement were quick to point out how, for an example, when we write something, we tend always use the male pronoun, "he" or "his", as in "Today's thinker is more profound than *his* predecessor". Or, "the average person looks forward to *his* salary". Without reflecting, we are supporting sexism by always using the male pronoun. One way to correct this tendency is to write "his/her" every time we need to write the pronoun. (When we get better at it, we may even rotate "his/her" to "her/his".)

This is not being pedantic because it reminds us how, without critical reflection, we can be sexist in our culture through the process of enculturation which we spoke about earlier. If we want to change our culture, we need to be attentive to what we say. Similarly, instead of referring to God as "he", we could stick with "God" since God is neither female nor male. We can also think of all the readings one hears at Mass that need overhauling and to be written in inclusive language. We can also start to use "pastor" instead of "priest" as a way to stress the pastoral role of the ordained and less focus on the cultic aspect. All this requires some effort and determination to break with the clerical and sexist past.

Unexamined assumptions

Other important aspects of clericalism are the unexamined assumptions that George Wilson has brought to our attention regarding clericalism. He says we should examine the basis of some of our attitudes. Clericalism thrives because of unexamined assumptions. We assume that because priests have studied many years, they know more than us on many matters. That may not be true. A simple Christian woman who has thought and prayed about the gospels may have more spiritual insight into a matter than the priest. A lay theologian may point our heresies that the priest is preaching from the pulpit. There are many assumptions about the ordained that we make without reflecting and questioning what we are thinking. Unfortunately we often act on these unexamined assumptions thus supporting clericalism.

In our stories, Margaret acted on the assumption that the parish priest would be able to give her an opinion on breastfeeding. Maria assumed that the parish priest would give her a sympathetic ear; in Canada parents of a child sexually assaulted by a priest went to see the bishop with the assumption that they would get a hearing. Instead he told them to see a lawyer; Annabel thought she would get the same recognition for a course that the males did; the parish priest that told a young woman not to wear slacks in HIS church assumed it was his church.

Here are some of these possible assumptions on the part of the ordained: "because I belong to the clergy I am automatically credible". The lay person might make this assumption: "he has a diploma on the wall so I can trust him". What further assumptions might be made about the titles people use, about showing respect for the cloth, about criticism of the priest, about the depth of his knowledge, about the ordained being quite different to the laity, about priests being better than lay people, about priests not having to be accountable because they are the shepherds of the flock; about priests driving large expensive cars?

You Speak, We Listen

Q: Do you agree that by remaining silent in the presence of clerical attitudes, one may be supporting clericalism? Say why you agree or disagree.

Q: Try to speak about your parish pastor without using "father". It will take some practice if you are like the rest.

Q: In calling your parish pastor "Juan" rather than "Father Gomez", are you showing disrespect? Explain yourself.

Q: Do you refer to the chair of your parish council as "John" or "Mr Goodenough"? Explain your choice.

Q: Choose some of the above assumptions related to clericalism and discuss them in your group. Analyse the assumptions one by one and see whether they are true or not.

Other opinions on clericalism

Let us now consider what others have said about clericalism. Cardinal Beniamino Stella is Prefect for the Congregation for the Clergy. He is forthright and speaks in a language we can understand:

> "Clericalism" is a word that has been on the Pope's lips a great deal in recent months. I think I am right

in saying that what the Holy Father means when he refers to the term "clerical" is that it describes the kind of priest who wants to give orders, who always thinks he knows best and becomes closed, hindering the mission of the Church. A clerical priest is a priest who withdraws into his own shell, into his own mindset and does not consult or listen to others, especially the laity, as he doesn't recognise the role of lay people in the Church's mission.

Sometimes, these kinds of priests believe they can dominate others, especially the poor and ignorant and that they belong to some kind of cast, claiming certain privileges and powers. "Clericalism" is bad for priests because it distorts their mission and is harmful for the laity because it hinders their development as adult Christians.

This word "clericalism" is a call to us priests to examine our consciences every day so that we don't forget that being clerics means being in a condition to bear witness to the faith in a more efficient way and show deep commitment to our vocation. Being a cleric does not give us some kind of social status that places up above others. This would create a gap between us. These are real risks for the pastoral ministry and we need to guard against them. To keep them at bay, we must keep our focus on the Cross, the humble and silent Virgin Mary who listens, suffers and gives herself. I hope everyone, myself included, can undertake this journey every day with God's help."[22]

---

22 Cardinal Beniamino Stella: "Let us not forget that a cleric's vocation brings him closer to people". By Andrea Tornielli, 18 February 2014. *Vatican Insider*.

You Speak, We Listen

Q: There are many issues raised in this passage by Cardinal Stella. Say which phrases or ideas caught your attention.

The *Royal Commission into Institutional Responses to Child Sexual Abuse* in Australia expressed their way of seeing clericalism in quite an extraordinary way. Here is the passage:

> Clericalism is the idealisation of the priesthood, and by extension, the idealisation of the Catholic Church. Clericalism is linked to a sense of entitlement, superiority and exclusion, and abuse of power." The report makes use of theological language that could well be exploited by those who see anticlericalism in this critique: The theological notion that the priest undergoes an "ontological change" at ordination so that he is different to ordinary human beings and permanently a priest, is a dangerous component of the culture of clericalism. The notion that the priest is a sacred person contributed to exaggerated levels of unregulated power and trust which perpetrators of child sexual abuse were able to exploit. Clericalism caused some bishops and religious superiors to identify with perpetrators of child sexual abuse rather than victims and their families, and in some cases led to denial that clergy and religious were capable of child sexual abuse. It was the culture of clericalism that led bishops and religious superiors to attempt to avoid public scandal to protect the reputation of the Catholic Church and the status of the priesthood. No

less damning is the report's characterisation of the governance of the Catholic Church.[23]

You Speak, We Listen

Q: The report says: "The report makes use of theological language that could well be exploited by those who see anticlericalism in this critique."

What does this sentence mean?

Q: "It was the culture of clericalism that led bishops and religious superiors to attempt to avoid public scandal to protect the reputation of the Catholic Church and the status of the priesthood."

Explain what is meant here.

Pope Benedict on clericalism

As we saw above, when Pope Benedict XVI came back to Rome after his visit to Cuba and Mexico in 2012, he was quite depressed by what he saw. In South America, the typical expressions of this clericalism include:

*Clergy see themselves as political powerbrokers, playing a direct role in affairs of state.

*The church projects an image of power and privilege, with its preferred spiritual imagery emphasising God as a cosmic monarch.

---

23 *The Final Report*, 15 December 2017.

*The role of the laity is conceived in largely passive terms – "pay, pray and obey".

*Little premium is placed on evangelisation or faith formation, with pastoral care understood largely in terms of administering the sacraments.

Here too the negative elements of clericalism are seen. The image of power and privilege, the passive role of the laity, lack of development in adult faith, clergy seeing themselves as political powerbrokers. The elements of clericalism seem to be universal.

One could take a more radical view of how people should be prepared for the ordained ministry today, but first we will critique the old seminary model. It was called seminary training, where "training" was the give-away word. Today, we need to talk about the preparation with greater educational insight.

Seminary system: think again

In traditional seminary training, other than theology, what time is given to topics like mediation, conflict management, learning the criteria for assessing people's gifts (pastors need to recognise the gifts that people have), interpersonal communication skills, the digital world? All these, and others, seem essential to the role of pastor. These should have a priority for the role of spiritual leader of the community. Alas, these topics have not been covered in the past, or, if attempted, the results have not been convincing.

It is time to reflect on the Orthodox tradition of preparing candidates for ordination. They make the distinction of what is necessary for the role of pastor as opposed to the role of theology professor. One should not expect one's pastor to be an academic theologian (we are all theologians once we speak of God). We expect our pastor to be a good pastoral person and spiritual director (and up to date with the directions of Vatican II). The role of teaching theology in a university or seminary is something else. It requires further specialised study at the Masters or doctoral level. (In the past, this has often been in Canon Law – a good qualification to have if the candidate is aiming at being a bishop one day!) In the Catholic Church, the two roles of pastor of a parish and theology professor are treated the same in the initial studies. This needs to change.

In a perceptive article, two former seminary professors in the United States have criticised the current system. The contents of this article apply at least to some other countries beyond English-speaking ones. They claim that seminaries have played a significant role in the current child sexual abuse cases. They further claim that seminary students are enculturated into clericalism from the moment they set foot in a seminary: "it is in the air they breathe". The career-climbers can be easily spotted by the fact that they are "learning Italian, wearing cufflinks and cassocks, and don't at all mind being called "Father," even though they are still in studies".[24]

The two professors moved on to issues relating to misogyny. They comment on the practice of separating men

---

24 C. Anderson and C. Bellitto, "The Reform Seminaries Need", *La Croix* 4 April, 2019. C. Colt Anderson, is professor of Christian Spirituality at Fordham University. He taught at Chicago's Mundelein Seminary (1999–2008) and Washington Theological Union, where he also served as the Vice President of Academic Affairs (2008–2012). He was a member of two seminary visitations in 2005. Christopher M. Bellitto, is professor of History at Kean University, and taught at New York's St Joseph's Seminary/Dunwoodie and its lay Institute of Religious Studies (1995–2001). He was part of a contentious layoff of faculty at Dunwoodie.

and women (as seminaries do) which can lead to hyper masculinity and which re-enforces the "otherness" of priests. Misogyny is rife in seminaries and their inability to relate to women is obvious. To cite the professors again: "It is the modern version of the ancient Madonna-whore complex. It only takes a few minutes of observing these men in social situations to realise many have no idea how to interact professionally with women."

> Or, as James Carroll, who has resigned from his ministry, puts it so bluntly:

> The Church's maleness and misogyny became inseparable from its structure. The conceptual underpinnings of clericalism can be laid out simply: Women were subservient to men. Laypeople were subservient to priests, who were defined as having been made "ontologically" superior by the sacrament of holy orders.[25]

The ambition of career students is reflected in their comments like, "When I'm pastor, I'm going to put my place on the map." (confirmed by Raimondo's story about the Sydney priest who was so excited by being given his parish, but was about to go on a skiing holiday). The professors noted, "We heard very little talk of service or shared leadership, collegial relations with parish councils, or facilitating the talents of parishioners. The parish, it was clear, belonged to the pastor and not the people". The seminarians are trained to be autocratic bosses, not servant leaders. The language used

---

25 James Carrol, "To Save the Catholic Church, Dismantle the Priesthood. Catholics must detach themselves from the clerical hierarchy and take the faith back into their own hand."This article appears in the June 2019 print edition of *THE ATLANTIC* with the headline "To Save the Church, Dismantle the Priesthood".

when a priest resigns from the ministry ("reduced to the lay state") is telling and reinforces clericalism.

This separation of pastor and people is clear in Pope Francis' words: "it (clericalism) alienates members of the Church by refusing to be close to them, and reinforces the belief that priests are above the laity".[26]

They (the professors) make a number of suggestions for reform.

- One suggested reform, then, is to make an explicit effort to keep seminarians as the lay people they are. The goal of a seminarian's path is ordination, but until ordination to the diaconate, that seminarian is a lay man. Why are they wearing cassocks and a Roman collar before then?

- Mix men and women, religious and lay in classes. The Synod on Youth's final document proposes: the joint formation of laity, consecrated religious and priests.

- The conclusion that "No priest is better than a bad priest" (11th century, St Peter Damien) suggests that a parish might have to wait without a priest for a while.

- The bishop should not be the only person to control seminaries.

- There needs to be a deliberative board consisting of members of the laity and religious that can regularly and independently audit the seminaries to ensure compliance with standards.

Not only does current seminary training encourage and promote clericalism, the introduction of foreign priests

---

26 Pope Francis, Vatican City, 13 December 2016, 04:50 pm (CNA/EWTN News).

to meet priest shortages can also promotes clericalism. If foreign priests are not thoroughly introduced to the culture they can cause great harm to the local parishioners. Why is this? Because they may well come from highly clericalised churches themselves that have not yet absorbed Vatican II. Catalysts for Renewal also raise the question of the justice of what this system does:

> Not only does the recruitment of priests from overseas prop up the culture of clericalism we have inherited, but this solution adopted by the church hierarchy perpetuates the very system of racial and economic injustice that the same church hierarchy seeks to challenge in its social teaching.[27]

You Speak, We Listen

Q: What has been your experience of seminaries, directly or indirectly?

Q: Do you agree with the authors' criticism of seminaries?

Q: Do you agree that seminaries promote clericalism?

Q: Explain the paragraph from Catalysts for Renewal about racial and economic injustice.

Preparation for Future Pastors

The above criticism raises the question of the preparation of candidates for ordination. We can call them "candidates", "ordinands" or "future pastors". There are a number of

---

27   Catalysts for Renewal, op.cit.

angles on this topic. What should the curriculum be? How, where, and with whom should it be taught? Where and how should the candidates' spiritual development be cared for? The first thing to say is that seminaries should be phased out, and space made for a "regenerated" ministry. "Regeneration" means new growth, as opposed to trying to patch up the old. We need a new paradigm, not a patched up old one, something more inspiring than the *The Gift of the Priestly Vocation*,[28] produced by the Congregation for the Clergy and which lacks this vision of regeneration.

I noticed that the above document did include a lot of Pope Francis' ideas, re the environment, clericalism, careerism, spirituality, ecumenism, other religions, psychology, anthropology, study of indigenous culture, learning a modern language, etc. These are all positive elements in the document but it does not go far enough. (I also noticed that it did *not* raise the basic question: what alternatives are there to a seminary preparation?)

Let us start with the curriculum. What might a renewed content look like? This should be revised and start from making the content much more universal, much more inclusive. Obviously there must be much in the curriculum relating to the Christian faith and Catholic tradition, but the large picture should form the backdrop.

It is possible today to attend a Mass and come out feeling that you have come out of a bubble which is unrelated to life outside. The ritual, the prayers, the words of the hymns, the theology, and especially the homily seem to come from a different world. (What a sharp contrast to Paul's letters that tackle real life situations.)

So what do I mean by "the large picture"? I mean some

---

28 Congregation for the Clergy, 8 December 2016.

understanding of the wonder and awe of creation. I mean the new cosmology, the possible universes, the latest research into the human person and how it functions (including understanding human sexuality), ethics, psychology (personality types) and psychiatry, an understanding of this planet in all its beauty and mystery and connectivity, quantum physics, the macro- and micro-world of quantum physics, and the whole digital world and human communications. The larger picture includes the sciences and humanities. This, you may think, is impossible for the individual but at least some appreciation of the modern understanding of these subjects is important if pastors are to communicate with all generations.

Thus a wider range of subjects should be studied from sciences and the humanities even though a certain prominence will be given to religion, philosophy, theology and liturgy. In particular, subjects that will aid pastoral work and provide pastors with the necessary skills relevant to this century, like mediation or conflict management skills, psychology, interpersonal communication skills, ethical reasoning and I.T. A first degree in the liberal arts with religion/theology as its majors is a possibility. Any such curriculum must have as its assumption that learning is a life-long activity.

How should these candidates learn? Modern ideas in how learning takes place and the stages and processes should be taken into account. Indoctrination is out. Best practice is in. Preparing people for the ordained ministry and other ministries should use the best models coming from theorists in contemporary education and then applied to different situations. First Order Learning (the basic facts, introduction to topics), Second Order Learning (critical reflective learning) and Third Order Learning (creative and transformational learning leading to possible shifts in paradigms) must all be used in the initial and ongoing education of pastors, if we want maturing adults in the ministry.[29]

The so-called Community of Inquiry, based on the ideas of Matthew Lipman (1923-2010, professor of education at Columbia University and founder of Philosophy for Children) and John Dewey (1859-1952, a professor of the Philosophy of Education), is another model that should be used. It is broadly defined as any group of individuals involved in a process of empirical or conceptual enquiry into problematic situations. This seems ideal for the many pastoral problems that face pastors in the twenty-first century. The three characteristics of this approach are (1) the problematic situation, (2) scientific attitude, and (3) participatory democracy. This approach has been adapted and used by others in a variety of educational situations.

Learn with whom?

For too long, seminarians studied by themselves in a hothouse seminary set apart from the rest of humanity. More recently, they have attended some colleges or theological unions, where lay men and women, ordained and lay, believers and others, also study and this is surely the path to follow. If there is no seminary in the future, then obviously they will learn at universities and colleges with a cross-section of students, male and female, and LGBT.

This is the ideal because it makes people aware of others and their opinions, belief systems and culture as well as their thinking processes. It will help to get rid of prejudices

---

29 Berise Heasly has an excellent chapter on this in her book, *Call No One Father*, op. cit., Chapter 5.

and biases, conscious and unconscious. This learning style, as opposed to indoctrination, opens the door for dialogue and debate which is always good if it stretches the mind and challenges our paradigms.

You Speak, We Listen

Q: To what areas of knowledge do you think future pastors need introduction?

Q: What areas of learning have you found helpful in your life's journey?

Q: What areas of learning have you found helpful in your faith development?

Q: If you were asked to think up an alternative method to seminaries for ordination preparation, what would you suggest?

Case 3

Abuse of power

Having considered the question of whose church it is, we can move on to discuss other angles on clericalism. Power is always a fascinating topic for discussion because of the way it can corrupt leaders, be they lay or ordained. We have only to look around us in society to see the way power is used and misused. As usual, we will start with someone's experience.

Chloe, a woman with many years experience in working with sacramental programs in parishes, writes on how off-hand their committee was treated.

> I was on a diocesan committee together with people from other parishes skilled in parish-based sacramental preparation to plan an inaugural Diocesan family-centred parish based sacramental program. But before we were anywhere near completing our planning the whole committee was discharged due to the appointment of a new bishop. I do not remember any real acknowledgment of our contributions except by the also discharged convenor. I was never thereafter consulted by the Diocese in any way concerning sacramental preparation.

I think we have an abuse of power here in this story. A bishop should treat the committees who work for the church with respect and value their contribution. The fundamental value we have as persons is to value the dignity and person of all others in the church (and beyond church). Ultimately, we are all children of God born equal. The way lay people are sometimes treated is a manifestation of the clericalism we are identifying. Pope Francis could have been speaking about Chloe in the above story when he said in one of his homilies about what he considers one of the great dangers of clericalism: that it alienates members of the Church by refusing to be close to them, and reinforces the belief that priests are above the laity.[30]

Valuing people

The least a new bishop (or new parish priest) could do would be to thank people who have contributed through committees and outline to them whether they continue or not in that capacity. To ignore people, to appoint a new committees without explaining procedures to the existing committee, is disgusting behaviour in society let alone in the church. But this does happen. How can this behaviour be reconciled with respecting the dignity of the person?

It seems the height of arrogance to treat people like non-persons by ignoring them or letting them find out that they are dismissed when they hear of a new committee.

One could add here the occasions when genuine, serious letters, emails or phone calls are not answered. Respect and common courtesy, let alone a common baptism, demand that people in authority (bishops, parish priests or parish council

---

30 Vatican City, 13 December 2016. ICNA/EWTN News.

chairs) respond to letters. Not doing so contradicts GS #3 and other paragraphs that talk about respect for others, thus making hypocrites of some hierarchs.

How could the bishop have acted differently? That answer seems simple. He could write to the members of the committee and thank them for their work, ask them if they would like to continue or explain the rules of selecting a new committee, or the length of term, and any other conditions, and explain how a new committee will be constituted. He could make people feel they are valued and understand the criteria and terms of office for future members. By not doing this, he is acting secretively which is one element of clericalism as we saw when defining the concept.

People's feelings must also be considered. Sadly, the number of psychopaths in positions of authority (in or outside the church) is significant (above the average across the population) and we know that they are insensitive to the feelings of others.

Chloe has another tale of abuse:

> Whilst preparing for an evening First Reconciliation, second rite liturgy, the assistant pastor, at the very last minute, changed many of the previously made arrangements for the liturgy against my advice as the co-ordinator. As the long-winded liturgy progressed extremely slowly, the result was tired children (the evening went on from 7pm to 10pm) angry and confused parents and other community members.

You Speak, We Listen

Q: *Imagine you are the bishop. You want to set up a new committee. What do you say to a member of the former committee?*

'Father-knows-best' syndrome

This is both a case of abuse of power and disregarding the advice of someone who knows. The parish priest is here treating his adviser with disdain, because he suffers from the "he knows best" syndrome, typical of clericalism.

The "father-knows-best" syndrome, can lead to excessive confidence and making judgments best left to God. Pope Francis has repeatedly said: you are not the judge; leave that for God to decide. This is one of the side-effects of clericalism – the tendency to know the mind of God and judge others. Chloe returns to this topic with this incident:

> Our State School catechetical team were forbidden by the pastor to invite the families in the state schools to sacramental preparation as the pastor perceived they were all "non- practising Catholics". It was only after a concerted effort by the catechists attending the parent evenings (without any state school parents in attendance), and representations made to the pastor by various catechists both by phone and in writing that he changed his mind and reluctantly allowed those children to prepare for and receive the sacraments.

The laity too can have this tendency to judge others as all are infected by clericalism. Teaching about the commandments and the rules of the Catholic Church easily led to people judging others according to these rules. With the emphasis on weekly Mass attendance, it was easy for Catholics to look around and judge who was absent and on the way to Hell. It should have been pointed out to us that we are not God. We do not decide who is "saved" and who is not.

Pope Francis has had much to say about clericalism, here he speaks about people like Chloe who feel discarded and abused.

> "The spirit of clericalism is an evil that is present in the Church today", Pope Francis said, "and the victim of this spirit is the people, who feel discarded and abused". That was the Pope's message in the homily at the morning Mass at the Casa Santa Marta.[31]

For a moment, let us move into the university situation. The following is an excerpt from a book by the Chinese scientist and reformer, Fang Lizhi, entitled, *The Most Wanted Man in China* (New York: Henry Holt and Company, 2016). It is about becoming a university vice president but could equally be applied to overworked pastors looking for reform:

> The first thing I learned was that many things didn't need any management. The university was full of educated people, and results were much better if you let people decide things for themselves than if you ran around trying to micromanage. Of course this meant that you couldn't flaunt your know-it-all 'leader' image. But if you were okay with that, it also meant that your workload fell by about 40 percent.[32]

---

31 Vatican Radio, *L'Osservatore Romano*, 13 December 2016.
32 p. 232.

You Speak, We Listen

Q: Can you think of any situations in life where you might attempt to micromanage?

Q: Why do you think some people like to micromanage?

Priests are not supermen or the "ontological" problem

There are many issues related to clericalism and we are working through them slowly. One that stands out like a pike above water is that of the claimed "ontological change" brought about in the priest at ordination. It is a theological opinion and probably does not directly concern most Catholics but they feel the effects and cannot deny its effectiveness in promoting clericalism.

The Royal Commission into Institutional Response to Child Sexual Abuse in Australia (2017) expresses the problem succinctly:

> The theological notion that the priest undergoes an "ontological change" at ordination so that he is different to ordinary human beings and permanently a priest is a dangerous component of the culture of clericalism. The notion that the priest is a sacred person contributed to exaggerated levels of unregulated power and trust which perpetrators of child sexual abuse were able to exploit.

There is a theological opinion that says that when a priest is ordained he becomes a different person, he undergoes an "ontological change". He becomes elevated about everyone else. He becomes a sort of superman. We all know that superman can take off his civilian clothes and fly from one building to another to rescue a person in distress. Young children like to put on their superman costume and pretend they can do marvellous things.[33] Clericalism too has had this effect in some cases.

Here we must go into the meaning of the word itself. The word we are talking about is ὄντος (in Greek) or *ontos*, meaning "being or that which is". The study of "being, existence" is called "ontology" which you would come across if you studied philosophy or theology. Indeed the idea of ontological change (and words like "transubstantiation" which also need re-visiting) come from medieval times and scholastic theology, exemplified by Thomas Aquinas.

For this century, we need to seek a different language to speak of these mysteries. Why is that? Because the meaning of words change, worldviews change with new knowledge and new understandings. Science is always discovering new ways of

---

[33] Interestingly the word "ontos" was given to a U.S. light armoured tracked anti-tank vehicle developed in the 1950s!!

understanding the way physics work on the macro and micro levels, symbols in language usage can become old and devoid of meaning. A symbol is used to describe something, perhaps a mystery, but over time that symbol might cease to speak to people; then it is time to look for new symbols. For example, the words "transubstantiation" and "consubstantial" have had their run and today mean little or nothing to people in the pews. It is pretty meaningless in today's world, to say that the ordained has undergone an "ontological change". The sexual abuse scandal in the church has robbed that claim of all content on a practical level.

You Speak, We Listen

Q: *Can you think of other church language or words used in old hymns, which has become meaningless for you?*

It was not until the 15th century that the notion that ordination confers an ontological change on the one ordained appeared in Catholic theology. It is comforting to know that this expression, "ontological change" does not appear in any official teaching of the Catholic Church. The Vatican II document, *Dogmatic Constitution on the Church*, section 10, articulated the issue with these words trying to explain the difference between ministerial priesthood (priest) and the common priesthood (lay person): : "Though they differ *essentially* [italics added] and not only in degree, the common priesthood of the faithful and the ministerial priesthood or hierarchical priesthood are none the less ordered to one another; each in its own proper way shares in the one priesthood of Christ." However, no one has explained what "differ essentially" means. Nor is the medieval wording of an "ontological change" any clearer. Ministerial priesthood makes sense to me when I see it more simply as: we all have a foundational calling to follow Christ and ordination is a further specification of that call.

What did Pope John Paul II say about this issue? He actually used the word *"ontological"* in his encyclical already cited (*Pastores Dabo Vobis*) but not "ontological change":

> It is as though the 1990 synod – rediscovering, by means of the many statements which we heard in this hall, the full depth of priestly identity – has striven to instil hope in the wake of these sad losses. These statements showed an awareness of the specific ontological bond which unites the priesthood to Christ the high priest and good shepherd. This identity is built upon the type of formation which must be provided for priesthood and then endure throughout the priest's whole life. This was the precise purpose of the synod. (#11)

One may well ask what is the ontological bond that unites the baptised with Christ the high priest? And, secondly, who were the people who developed, and now popularise, his theology of ontological change?

Later on in this encyclical, he returns to this point without actually mentioning ontological change, but refers to "spiritual power" that flows from an ontological and psychological bond between Christ and the priest:

> By sacramental consecration the priest is configured to Jesus Christ as head and shepherd of the Church, and he is endowed with a "spiritual power" which is a

share in the authority with which Jesus Christ guides the Church through his Spirit.(#21)[34]

Interesting enough, John Paul II also wants to say, in the same encyclical, that the priest is human although he has an "ontological bond" which unites the priesthood to Christ. He cites the letter to the Hebrews. He states:

> The Letter to the Hebrews clearly affirms the "human character" of God's minister. He comes from the human community and is at its service, imitating Jesus Christ "who in every respect has been tempted as we are, yet without sin" (Hebrews 4:15).

It might well be safer to stick with the New Testament than medieval philosophical wording. The New Testament speaks of the importance of baptism, the coming down of the Holy Spirit and the Eucharist, but not about the spiritual status of those who are his disciples or those who preside at the Eucharist.

The *Catechism of the Catholic Church* (CCC) states that ordination "confers an indelible spiritual character" which "cannot be repeated or conferred temporarily" (CCC#1583). "The vocation and mission received on the day of his ordination mark him permanently" (CCC#1583). The nature of this "indelible spiritual character" is not explained.

The impact of this indelible character might well be worth thinking about in terms of how the official church, having placed the ordained on a high pedestal, has treated priests who have dared to resign their ministry. They have been banned from several ministries in the local church and belittled in many ways by the hierarchy. Is the Catholic Church the only church that shoots its wounded soldiers? Is

---

34   *Pastores dabo vobis*, #21.

this the result of the clericalism we are investigating? I think it is.

Nowhere in the New Testament do we see Jesus do or say anything that would support this revengeful attitude. Jesus never retaliates if someone does not follow him or needs time out. In many Christian churches, they understand that some ministers need to resign for a variety of reasons, personal or professional. In these cases, the ministers concerned receive understanding and empathy. Not so in the official Catholic Church.

Although "ontological change" in not in official documents from Vatican II, there are some people who continue to support it. It is difficult to locate in writing although more conservative theologians might use it. This is especially so in modern times. There are some instances one can cite, like the following words of the conservative Cardinal John O'Connor of New York who dares to make a comparison between priests and the Eucharist:

> During the International Reunion of Priests in Fatima on 18 June 1996, John Cardinal O'Connor spoke on *"The Necessity of Continuing Formation for the Priest."* He stated:
>
> *"In my judgment, this concept of the ontological nature of the priesthood is critical. We don't just put on vestments; we don't just receive an assignment. Neither makes us priests. We become priests at ordination. There is an "ontological change" in our spiritual nature. Such is a profound mystery. Is it too bold an analogy to compare the change to Christ the Son of God's retaining*

> *His Divinity while becoming a man? Or to observe that after bread becomes the Sacred Body of Christ, it still tastes like bread and feels like bread, but is now the Body of Christ? There has been an ontological change. A cup of wine still smells like wine and tastes like it, but it is now the Blood of Christ. At ordination an ontological change takes place."*[35]

It is not easy to find theologians using this expression in written form but here is one from Australia. Dr Marie Keenan, giving evidence to the Royal Commission into Institutional Responses to Child Sexual Abuse, has researched the statement of Julian Porteous, Archbishop of Hobart, about this ontological change. She writes thus:

> In a programme on ABC National Radio in Australia, the following extract from a book on priesthood published in 2008 and written by Bishop Porteous, an Australian bishop and until 2008 Rector of an Australian Seminary in Sydney, illustrates succinctly the point I wish to make. Bishop Porteous describes the changes that occur at ordination.
>
> *A man once ordained is ontologically changed. He is a priest. Something mysterious happens. It is an action of grace, and something quite real... The priesthood is not just the deputing of an individual to take on a particular role. It is more than a function; it is a radical reorienting of the whole reality of the person. He is changed at the level of his being... Ordination is not just the power to exercise the priestly office in the Church; it is such a*

---
[35] https://www.catholicdoors.com/faq/1000/qu1329.htm accessed on 30.10.2019.

transformation of the person that a distinctly priestly character can be identified in him.[36]

You Speak, We Listen

Q: Does Jesus ever speak about those who will preside at future Eucharists?

Q: Why do you think this ministry has become so dominant in the life of the church?

Criticism of "ontological change"

As we implied above, no reputable theologian would support it today. Yet a few do speak of it and those who support clericalism in theory and practice would welcome this argument to maintain the *status quo*. In fact, the average parishioner probably has never heard of "ontological change" but knows the practice of it.

The Plenary Report, already cited, expresses the implications of this high priesthood theology very accurately:

> We defined clericalism as an attitude among laity and ordained that the ordained is somehow superior, 'above', worthy of more respect, has an entitlement to more authority, a power of veto over lay decisions as desired, less accountability and less transparency in decision-making than the non-ordained are entitled to by virtue of their Baptism.[37]

---

[36] J. Porteous, *After the Heart of God: The Life and Ministry of Priests at the Beginning of the Third Millennium*. (Ballan, Australia: Connor Court Publishing, 2008). https://www.childabuseroyalcommission.gov.au/sites/default/files/IND.0675.001.0001.pdf accessed 24 November 2019.

[37] ACBC, *Listening to what the Spirit is Saying*, op.cit., 80.

Let me give an example: when a friend of mine was ordained, his mother quietly told my mother, that now that her son was ordained, we (his mates) should no longer call him "Barry" but "Father Barry". (He has left the ordinary level of human beings and had undergone an ontological change to arrive at a superior level of existence.) We ignored this advice and continued to call him the way we knew him, simply "Barry". After all, Jesus never asked anyone who followed him to be addressed in a special way as a result of his commitment.

This sort of thinking is miles away from what Jesus spoke about in the Gospels and his idea of being the servant of everyone.

According to those who still use the medieval philosophical terms, the idea of an "ontological change" in the ordained is that, in his being, he becomes different. We need to put this way of talking into the context of clericalism in the church to give us some perspective. Theology develops over time. The practice comes first and then the theology follows. After Constantine, the image and status of the ordained grew in importance in the eyes of many. The status of the ordained was greater than the peasant because the former had some education and dealt in holy things. The theology of priesthood followed but it was not until the fifteenth century that this idea of ontological change took hold. And it is no surprise that those who developed this high theology were the ordained themselves.

Given the clericalism that exists in the church, this theology of ontological difference gives support to the idea that the ordained is superior in status, on a different level to the rest. The relationship between clericalism and a high theology of priesthood is symbiotic, that is, they are mutually supportive. Those priests who support John Paul II and his theology of priesthood welcome the idea of ontological change because it supports their high theology of priesthood. It is a great way of re-enforcing a position of power over people, to tell them that they are ordinary beings but you are a super being. This flatly contradict the gospels about ministry.

You Speak, We Listen

This question relates to the last paragraph above.

Q: Had there been prominent women theologians in the church, would there ever had been such a high theology of priesthood? Give reasons for your reply.

The ontological change theory has no basis in Scripture and makes no sense other than to support clericalism. Our priesthood, be it lay or ordained, has its basis in the priesthood of Christ and leave it like that. It might be better today to say that ordination places one in another position (i.e. order or group) in the community, not a better or more privileged place, but a place from which one is called to spend one's life exclusively in service of the people of God.[38]

What is of far more practical concern today is the role of the ordained in the community, the encouragement of lay ministries, and the realisation of co-responsibility for the mission, which is the church. Pope Francis has said it plainly, referring to *Apostolicam Actuositatem*, that this council

---

[38] https://bustedhalo.com/questionbox/can-you-explain-what-haparish priestens-at-ordination-when-the-ontological-change-haparish priestens. Richard J. Malloy S.J. accessed 30.10.2019.

document indicated that the work of the church is meant to be undertaken by all." [39]

Joshua McElwee refers to a letter from Pope Francis to Cardinal Ryiko:

> "This document has recalled with force that... the proclamation of the Gospel is not reserved to some 'mission professionals' but should be the deep yearning of all lay faithful, called, in virtue of their baptism, not only to the Christian animation of temporal realities, but also to the explicit works of evangelisation, proclamation and sanctification of peoples," states Francis.[40]

The servant model is the antidote

The Gospel approach to ministry is that of the servant model. Jesus speaks about being the servant of all. There was a time in the church when the pope used the title "Servant of the servants". Unfortunately other titles like "Vicar of Christ" and "Pontifex" also arose. And cardinals became "princes" of the church, and bishops "Lords" or "Your Grace", or " Your Excellency". Pope Francis has repeated reminded us all that Catholic pastors are called to serve the laity, not the other way around.

The clothing that hierarchs wear is often a dead give-away. The dresses that hierarchs use today are symbols of power and contradict the servant image found in the Gospels. Let us consider what the Gospels say.

---

39 Joshua McElwee, A letter from Pope Francis addressed to Cardinal Rylko on the 50th Anniversary of *Apostolicam Actuositatem*.
40 Ibid.

In describing the hypocrisy of (some) of the Scribes and Pharisees, Jesus says the disciples should do as they say but not as they do. They do not practice what they preach. Jesus has something to say about ostentatious dressing to attract attention. He observed (Matthew 23:5) how some Jews wore large phylacteries (the little boxes containing the words of Yahweh in them, from Deuteronomy and Leviticus) on their foreheads to show off and had long fringes or tassels, on their tallit (prayer shawl).

One thinks of the elaborate and colourful dresses, hats, rings, shoes, that some bishops and cardinals wear, including the cappa magna, the long flowing cape like a wedding train that some cardinals still wear. For some people, this is what comes to mind when they think of clericalism:

> Some also associated it with the ornate vestments – "the outward trappings, the outrageous garb" – worn by bishops and cardinals. Clericalism was seen by many as preventing others from "being the Church". A number of people spoke of it as "authoritarianism", "careerism" or "misogyny" and believed that it gave priests an exalted and exclusive status that was detrimental to both the priest and the community.[41]

Retired Bishop Cullinane of New Zealand has some sobering thoughts on symbolism and garb. He saw a significant shift from one model of exercising authority to another. This raises questions about the symbols of authority inherited from the previous model. On entering the clerical state, the tonsure and skullcap were given, which signified apartness and privilege.

---

41   ACBC, "Listen to what the Spirit is Saying", op cit, 80.

Today, priests no longer wear the black skullcap, but use of the purple and scarlet skullcaps to signify "higher rank" lingers on. The mitre had been part of the uniform of officials at the imperial court in fifth century Byzantium. The shepherd's crook could aptly replace both those insignia. At least it has a biblical allusion. The title "Excellency" which is still used by Roman Congregations to address bishops, was given in 1930 when Pope Pius XI wanted to match Mussolini's gesture of giving that title to his mayors. Some cling to these insignia and titles precisely to signify the kind of authority they originally signified. Some find them incompatible with Jesus' teaching in Matthew 23:1-10. Some regard them as harmless embellishments. Some shrug them off as "toys for the boys". Others see them as left-overs from models of authority that the Church is being called to move away from. Perhaps others are waiting for someone else to make the decision for them.[42]

The biblical response to titles is clear. Jesus was against titles. He said "call no one your father except God in heaven".

Disciples are to model themselves on the ministry of Jesus who was humble and committed to his ministry. His whole life was given over to healing others, to comforting them, to speaking to ordinary people, to fulfilling his role as a Jewish prophet in the line of Amos, Isaiah, Hosea and Jeremiah and the others; and encouraging others to fulfil the Law of Deuteronomy and Leviticus, that is, to Love of God and their neighbour as themselves.

---

[42] Peter Cullinane, "A Matter of Style", Vatican Media, I June 2019. Peter Cullinane is Bishop Emeritus of Palmerston North, New Zealand. This article was originally published in NZ Catholic Newspaper (Issue 564, May 5-18 2019).

Cardinal de Aviv has said the following regarding the theme of servant. He is currently Prefect of the Congregation for Religious Life. Joshua McElwee reports:

> Pope Francis is calling on Catholic priests and clergy around the world to stop seeking positions of power or authority and to instead "lower themselves" in service to the poor and those most in need, Cardinal João Braz de Aviz has said. The Brazilian prelate, who leads the Vatican's office for religious life, said: "We of the clergy must lower ourselves... we consecrated must lower ourselves because we are too high", "We, in many important posts, must lower ourselves, most of all changing the rules that guide us", said the cardinal. "Not being any more 'number one' or making an 'upgrade' always to the better position, but realising a fraternal Church... in which, truly, the smallest, the poor, those that are thrown away, feel called, feel loved and we are with them." Braz de Aviz was speaking on Saturday at an event celebrating the Pact of the Catacombs, a symbolic agreement made among some 40 global bishops at the end of the Second Vatican Council to live and work for a "Church of the poor."[43]

The importance of synodality

In his struggle against clericalism, Pope Francis has repeatedly not only spoken of, but moved in the direction of synods. Synods are all about dialoguing with all in the church, and thus undercuts the arrogant, clerical, "father-knows-best" attitude.

---

43 Joshua McElwee, *Vatican Insider*, 19 November 2015.

Throughout the world, the Catholic Church is planning, or have already had, a Synod or Plenary Council to review how their local church is doing. Certainly since Vatican II, synods have occurred more frequently although some are becoming disillusioned by the way they have been managed. By this, I mean under Pope John Paul II and Pope Benedict, the participants were sent home after the synod and it was left to the Pope to publish his own statement on the synod topic which may, or may not, correspond to what the synod wanted. The lack of lay participant with voting rights is another cause for caution.

Let me give two examples of recent synods. In Rome, Pope Francis called the Synod for the Amazon (2019) to discuss the serious exploitation of the rainforests in the context of climate change. In Australia, the bishops called for a Plenary Council (2020) in the light of the Royal Commission into Institutional Responses to Child Sexual Abuse which found that 7% of priests were involved in sexual abuse of children. Other countries will have their own agenda although sexual abuse seems to have been fairly universal. The calling of these councils, under Pope Francis, is a sign of a change in method, that is, listening to the people.

The aim of these synods or plenary councils (there are technical differences) is to give a voice to all in the church, in contradistinction to the past when ordinary parishioners were expected to do as they were told, or, as the cynical slogan went, "to pray, pay and obey". So the new direction is to invite parishioners to speak their mind. The Pope has asked his bishops too to say what they think, not what they think the Pope wants to hear!! Thus with synods and Plenary Councils, individuals are asked to speak up and participate in a process that will obviously have a few stages. The danger is that their voices might be lost in the stages, either intentionally or unintentionally, because, as we all know, there is a minority of those in the church who want to return to the pre-Vatican II church, and reject the reforms and renewal that Pope Francis has embraced.

Let me introduce a new phrase used in this context. And then I will relate it to synodality and the laity. It is *sensus fidei* (Latin), which is one's understanding of faith, one's instinct of faith. It is used in the singular. How do you understand a particular matter of faith? Let me quote a more formal explanation:

> The *sensus fidei* is a sort of spiritual instinct that enables the believer to judge spontaneously whether a particular teaching or practice is, or is not, in conformity with the Gospel and with apostolic faith.[44]

It is not a rational solution to a question but an instinct, a form of spontaneous knowledge. So if somebody asked you: is euthanasia allowed by your religion, you might respond quickly without a rational discussion. Or if somebody asked you: is capital punishment wrong?, you will respond according to your instinct.

There is a second phrase used in this connection and it is the ecclesial form of the previous phrase, *sensus fidei*. It is *sensus fidelium*, that is the "feeling, or sense of the faithful". It refers to the faithful, all the people. However, it is not just the popular vote on an issue. *Sensus fidelium* implies prayer and thoughtful consideration, discernment, in the light of the Gospels.

This fine idea and teaching was buried for centuries because, as one can easily see, it does not fit in with the

---

[44] International Theological Commission, *Sensus Fidei in the Life of the Church*, London: Catholic Truth Society, 2014, 31.

authoritarian, monarchical model of church governance of the past centuries. No bishop or Pope was particularly interested in what the parishioners thought. (And hence bishops were appointed who could enforce the teachings, not ask for opinions!). Pope Francis, however, is talking about a new model of governance. In this model the emphasis is on all voices being heard, which signals what some people call "a shift in paradigm".

Vatican II emphasised the teaching about the instinct of faith, because it valued the role that every baptised Christian plays in the church. The council taught that all the baptised participate in the three offices of Christ as prophet, priest and king (we will explain these three later). So Christ fulfils his prophetic office not only through the hierarchy but also through the laity. This is a great step forward from the clerical attitude of Christ communicating only through the hierarchy.

As it is a new model, we can flag a new problem: most bishops and most of the laity are not used to being asked their opinion, so it might take some time to change direction. I like to think of it as trying to turn a fast-moving aircraft carrier around. It cannot be done quickly. In Australia, the bishops, through the ACBC, encouraged inclusive participation. The ACBC website says, "All comments and feedback are invited". Everyone is encouraged "to discover how you can be a part of the Australian Plenary Council journey".[45] The challenge is going to be how to bring this about. Here we can point out that clericalism does just the opposite; it discourages participation, or, in the words of Pope Francis, "Clericalism, far from inspiring various contributions and proposals, gradually extinguishes the prophetic flame of which the

---

45 First joint Plenary Meeting. Monday 23 October 2017. ACBC website.

entire Church is called to bear witness in the heart of her peoples".[46]

Let me return to the idea of synod. The word "synod" comes from the Greek word, "synodos"[47] meaning "walking with" or "on the path together", and it is synonymous with the Latin word for council, which is *concilium*.[48] In the early centuries of church history, synods were meetings of bishops (not necessarily with the Pope), and the word is still used in that sense in Catholicism, Oriental Orthodoxy and Eastern Orthodoxy. A term similar to synod is Plenary Council which means a meeting of the church including everyone, that is, clergy, religious and laity (The Anglican and Orthodox Churches have had this type of inclusive synod for many years).

We read about a variety of regional or episcopal synods in the first centuries of Christianity, both East and West. Here are a few of these councils which show a distribution across the Mediterranean: Rome (155), Ephesus (193), Carthage (251 and 311), Iconium (258), Antioch (264), Elvira (Spain, near modern Granada, 306), Neo-Caesarea (314). It became clear that with so many councils meeting and all making some rules, or "canons" as they call them, co-ordination was necessary to bring some order in the Christian Church.

The Synod of Serdica (343 CE, modern day Sofia, Bulgaria) tried to do this by trying to establish Rome as the reference point for decisions in difficult matters. This was eventually done by the Council of Nicaea (325 CE) which came together to establish a central council that could sort all the different canons (rules) that had been passed by smaller councils throughout the church. Athanasius argued

---
46 26 April 2016. *NCR*.
47 σύνοδος (sýnodos).
48 "concilium"

that Nicaea alone enjoyed proper authority and inspiration, with the right to demand loyalty of all true Christians. Pope Damasus in the fourth century, claimed that the unique authority of the council of Nicaea rested on the fact that Pope Silvester had approved it.

In the West, regional bishops would write to Rome requesting decisions on certain matters in imitation of secular society where the provincial governors would write to the emperor for guidance. It is interesting, from our point of view today at the beginning of the 21st century, what these issues were. We might well be surprised. They were "the age and qualifications of candidate for Holy Orders, the degrees of kindred and affinity that constitute a bar to Christian marriage, and the need for requiring celibacy in bishops, priests and deacons". [49]

In the East, the Christian churches, centred on Constantinople, were less inclined to look to Rome for guidance so that the synodal method of addressing issues developed more independently and securely than in the West. That might also explain why the Orthodox churches today have such strong bases in their patriarchates. The churches in the West soon came under Rome and, following the Roman Empire as a template, became very centralised. Hence our problem today with trying to introduce synodality as a new way to operate in the Catholic Church. Pope Benedict was at first keen to de-centralise and give some authority to Episcopal Conferences, but then hesitated and abandoned the idea. Pope Francis is trying to re-visit the idea.

The synodality emphasis will help to minimise clericalism in so far as it shows that all in the church have

---

49 Henry Chadwick, *The Early Church*, Harmondsworth: Penguin Books, 1967, 240.

something to offer and are equal in this regard. It rejects the element in clericalism which implies that the ordained have all the truth and knowledge or that the Holy Spirit only works through the ordained.

You Speak, We Listen

Q: Have you had any experience of been consulted in your parish on any issues?

Q: Have you had any experience of synods or diocesan assemblies? Describe it to the group.

Q: Are you in favour of this kind of consultation? Give your reasons.

Case 4

Infantilising the laity

By the expression "infantilising the laity", I mean treating the laity like children. Pope Francis has often mentioned this behaviour in his talks. Here Chloe again writes of her experience:

> Whilst working within a parish, the pastor had reluctantly appointed a Parish Council but told me gleefully, that as they would only meet monthly the council would not interfere with his plans for the parish or the status quo. He said that they would all be too disorganised to have time to introduce anything they (the new parish council) thought important.

There are two other stories we can mention here. Again the writer is Chloe:

> Many others within our parish community have told me that "Father should be asked'" before I and other team members introduce any simple changes or additions. Even though the team in question has the knowledge, experience and should have the authority to do so.

Here is an example of lay person-to-lay person which is important because clericalism is not only seen in ordained-lay relationships. Jocasta is a woman of many years experience in parish life. She pinpoints an important point:

> When a lay person was asked to say a few words (having had time to prepare it) at a Sunday Eucharist, he waffled on for more than ten minutes with so much incorrect historical knowledge that members of the congregation were obviously embarrassed. I walked out as I have done to many an episcopal person in my day, for the same reason.

Lay people can be guilty of clericalism

Here we have the example of a lay person-to-lay person relationship. Lack of adequate preparation for his reflection is an insult to the parishioners and is treating them like children. The person in Jocasta's story should be obliged to make sure he is prepared and his information is accurate out of respect for his parishioners. Treating them without respect like children is a dimension of clericalism. There is a danger also that those preparing for the permanent diaconate take on the clerical attitudes of priests they have known. If the clerical attitude is the only example they know, there is a great chance they will mimic that attitude. Lay people are just as vulnerable to clericalism as the ordained. Jocasta's example is a good one to show that clericalism occurs in the lay-to lay relationship as well as the more obvious ordained-lay relationship.

I do recall a parish priest who repeated his 3-year cycle of homilies without any updating. This was pretty obvious in his Trinity Sunday homily which quickly came down to "well the Trinity is a mystery so what can we say?"

The laity are intelligent beings. Many are better educated than the pastor. Regarding decision-making they should be allowed to make decisions where possible (the principle of subsidiarity). Chloe reflects the disrespect for the laity where the pastor has become authoritarian:

> I have had to ask the pastor's approval many times to introduce usually simple or minor changes. Obviously more radical changes that I thought were needed would be introduced after consultation with the pastor and others.

Chloe would agree with the sentiment from the Plenary Council Report which sets the ideal: "What is God asking of us: That the ordained (priest, bishop) work alongside and with others, be seen as an equal and have an equal place at the table when it comes to decisions. That the gifts, talents and leadership skills of all the People of God be recognised, utilised and respected, whether ordained or not".[50]

Pope Benedict has said, "It is not right for them to feel treated like second-class citizens in the church... despite the committed work which they carry out in accordance with their proper vocation, and the great sacrifice which this dedication at times demands of them".[51]

You Speak, We Listen

Q: Can you recall any such incidents when you have felt you were treated like a child ?

---

50 ACBC, "Listen to what the Spirit is Saying", op.cit., 80.
51 John Allen, "Benedict's gentle debunk of clericalism", 30 March 2012.

The principle of subsidiarity

By the principle of subsidiarity, I mean that people should be able – within an organisation – to make decisions at their level and expertise. A nurse who knows her job well will be able to make certain judgments regarding her patients without having to refer to the doctor. If the doctor is not happy with that, they might need to discuss which decisions are fine for her to make and which not. A teller in a bank should be able to make some decisions in his workplace without running to the CEO for every little decision. That shows respect for the expertise and ability of the teller. Likewise in a parish, parishioners should be free to make decisions within their area of responsibility and expertise which shows respect for all in the church as they are all baptised Christians. The pivotal sacrament is baptism, not ordination.

Another story worth being told is that of Andy McAlpin about his uncle. It refers to treating people as adults and listening to what they have to say.

> Possibly the best example from my life that explains clericalism is the story of my great uncle. He was a highly educated and intelligent man who, according to his children, wanted to believe. He came from a strong Irish Catholic background. When Uncle Thomas met with his local parish priest many decades ago, he mentioned to him some of the books he was reading and told the priest that he was questioning his faith. Instead of listening to Uncle Tom's concern and his story, all the priest did was tell him that it was a sin to read those books. That's it. Case closed. Uncle Tom left

the Church, never to return, yet never being hostile to those of faith.[52]

I had a similar incident when discussing religious matters with a Jehovah's Witness over the garden fence one Saturday morning. We got talking and soon I realised he was Italian by birth. He explained to me that although he was born a Catholic, when, later in life, he questioned the parish priest about issues in the Bible, he got the infantilising reply that he should not worry his head about such matters.

Pope Francis on infantilisation

Pope Francis rejects the infantilisation of the laity and supports their true mission, as the following incident makes clear. In Brazil, Francis led the bishops through an examination of conscience, which included the question: Do we give the laity "the freedom to continue discerning, in a way befitting their growth as disciples, the mission which the Lord has entrusted to them? Do we support them and accompany them, overcoming the temptation to manipulate them or infantilise them?"[53] He continued: "Being a cleric does not give us some kind of social status that places up above others. This would create a gap between us. These are real risks for the pastoral ministry and we need to guard against them."

The way the laity are treated is part of clericalism. The Pope warns us that clericalism "nullifies the personality of Christians" and it also "leads to the functionalisation of the laity, treating them as 'errand boys [or girls]'."[54] The Pope has asked for the "essential role" of the laity to be "reinforced"

---
52 McAlpin, op.cit.
53 "The Church is more than the Pope", Thomas Reese. *NCR*, 16 January 2015.
54 Ines San Martin, "Pope blasts Clericalism", *Crux*, 27 April 2016.

so that they take on "the responsibilities that they have". Lay people "have an authentic Christian formation and should not need a bishop-pilot, a monsignor-pilot, or clerical input in taking on their own responsibilities on all levels, from the political to the social level, from the economic to the legislative level! Everyone, however, is in need of a pastor bishop!"[55]

The infantilisation of the laity is well captured in this humourous and critical poem, The Bureaucrat's Prayer. Although it is the prayer of a bureaucrat, it could well be the prayer of the laity pre-Vatican II.

One can note its themes and think of how they could well reflect the Catholic Church of the past. The laity are expected to comply with regulations (like fasting from midnight before communion). It mentions mindless compliance with rules, to accept rules and regulations without using our common-sense, not to plan for the future (I know of one diocese where planning for the future was forbidden); to suppress initiative (and the Holy Spirit); to obey without reasoning the absence of accountability; and the desire to be like a flock of compliant sheep because this is what God wants.

The Bureaucrat's Prayer

Oh, Thou, who seest all things below
Grant that Thy servant may go slow;
That we may study to comply
With regulations till we die.

Teach us, O Lord, to reverence
Committees more than common-sense;

---

[55] Pope Francis, "House of God refuge, not prison", *Vatican Insider*, 20 May 2015.

Impress our minds to make no plan
And pass the baby when we can.

And when the Tempter seems to give
Us feelings of initiative,
Or when, alone, we go too far
Recall us with a circular.

Mid fire and tumult, war and storms,
Sustain us, Blessed Lord, with forms,
Thus may they servants ever be
A flock of perfect sheep for Thee.

The lesson we learn from Jocasta's story of the lay preacher above, is that we should always be well prepared – if giving a reflection or homily – out of respect to those to whom we are speaking. Just because a person is a deacon or chair of the parish council, does not mean they can go into a speech or meeting unprepared. Think of the people who are the audience and the fact that they are well educated and adults, and might have well developed critical faculties. So be prepared! This is the way to avoid infantilising the laity, or your audience.

Pope Francis has pointed out the effects of clericalism with regard to the laity.

> Clericalism leads to a homogenisation of the laity; treating it as an 'emissary' limits the various initiatives and efforts and, I dare say, the boldness necessary to be able to bring the Good News of the Gospel to all areas of social and above all political activity. Clericalism, far from inspiring various contributions and proposals,

gradually extinguishes the prophetic flame to which the entire Church is called to bear witness in the heart of her peoples.[56]

At the heart of this is the role of the laity about which much has been written and little applied, in my experience. I think there is the possibility of talking too much about it at the expense of doing something. That is why lay people need to request action. They need to protest as Luther and his supporters did in the sixteenth century, but this time the clergy must listen and not wait five hundred years to do something about it. The laity have a big influence on the outcomes of reform, of getting rid of clericalism since without their co-operation, clericalism would die out or churches become empty (as some are already doing).

Bishop Cullinane stresses how things have changed over centuries, and in today's world the dignity of the individual has come to the fore. He refers to the new style of handling change used by Pope Francis and explores its roots:

> But the needed change of style has deeper roots. It is based on what it means to be a person, and what it means to fully respect the primacy of conscience. A deeper appreciation of what these mean has been growing in the Western world over many years, and has been gradually recognised in the Church. It is less evident in the Churches of the East. And it is non-existent wherever "religion" is still promoted by force or fear. It is a development that was both acknowledged and affirmed by the Second Vatican Council: The dignity of the human person is a concern

---

56 Address to participants in the Pontifical Commission for Latin America plenary assembly, April 26, 2016. NCR, Feb 17, 2017.

of which people of our time are becoming increasingly more aware. In growing numbers people demand that they should enjoy the use of their own responsible judgment and freedom and decide on their actions on grounds of duty and conscience, without external pressure or coercion.[57]

Co-responsibility

The laity must assume a role of *co-responsibility* as the late Cardinal Martini used to say. They will find this difficult as traditionally, they are used to being passive and told what to do and not to do anything without permission. It is my intuition that many Catholics today do not really want to do more than go to Mass and put something in the collection basket. These actions are the minimum required for salvation (in their thinking). Or, to put it another way, going to church on Sundays is seen as a kind of "fire insurance".

Not too many seem prepared to re-think their religious commitment in terms of what the gospel wants and then re-construct their role as co-responsible with the clergy for the mission which is the church. The church does not "have a mission"– the church "is mission". When the church nationally has a separate building and staff for "Catholic Mission", it sends the unintended message that parishes are not missions!! Perhaps this too has contributed to some parishes being concerned more with maintenance rather than mission. Again, as we saw above, Pope Francis sets us right in stressing that mission should be the deep yearning of all the faithful.

---

57 Cullinane, op.cit.

The desire to clericalise everyone

The ordained and the lay person both have their respective roles to play. It is pointless trying to drive everyone into the clerical group since the groups have distinct functions. One way to fight clericalism is precisely to dissuade the hierarchy from trying to clericalise the laity. Consider the following:

1) Should women become deacons in the church? The Pope does not seem keen on the idea because it only sends women down the path of clericalism. Better, if within the church, there were positions for women that carried decision-making ability. This would give them a say in the church without turning them into clerics.

   Some women have rejected the idea of becoming priests because they do want to be forced into a model of priesthood that they reject. If the model were to change into a non-clerical model (one that rejects clericalism), perhaps they would welcome ordination. But is it possible to have a non-clerical model for the clergy? It sounds like a contradiction in terms. Perhaps we can only hope for a less clerical model, or a model without the worst features of clericalism and which we can call "pastoral".

2) Now we can consider men. Should good male parishioners be funnelled into the path that leads to deacons, and thus clericalises them? Instead, they could have decision-making roles within the community without being clerics. This is impossible while the parish priest has all the decision-making power.

Some years ago, a friend of mine who had contributed much to the local church, was approached by the parish priest and asked if he would like to be a senior server? He rejected this offer because he saw it as an introduction to the path that would lead to clericalism. Lay people should have their legitimate role as lay people within the church.

Here is a further thought that marginalises the laity. A defence of clericalism used by some in the church is the following argument: that lay people are a "bridge between the church and the world". The laity work in the world, not in the church. So they must be kept from decision-making roles in the church. Do not let the laity usurp power in the church. This argument is calculated to protect the power of the clergy. It is a dualistic view of the world. Both ordained and lay are in the world and in the church. All Christians, ordained or lay, should be a bridge between the church and the world.

There is a danger that many of the laity will be drawn into being clericalised and when that occurs, they will follow the model they know and see – the clerical model. The following story is the case of two men who became permanent deacons. Jocasta tells the story:

> At a Eucharist with a group of ecumenical staff, the Permanent Deacon told non-Catholic staff members that they were not to go to Communion. He acted as though he was the celebrant at any Eucharist he attended and was taken aback when not given the respect he 'deserved' as a quasi member of the clerical cast. And yet he also had issues with the real clerics when they displayed clericalism!
>
> Somehow the office of permanent deacon needs some clear guidelines to prevent certain lay persons

from achieving their life's dream to be a cleric! I have taught Deacons and seen what happened with two different men at their Ordination. Their speeches at the ceremony told the whole story of how each saw their ministry of service. The behaviour, relayed by parishioners, of the one displaying pure clericalism, has shown that he should never have been ordained.

You will recall that this preoccupation with status was one of the elements in clericalism as seen in the definition of clericalism in Case 1 above. The theologian Stanley Hauerwas reminds us: "Jesus called his followers, the disciples, not from the elites of this world but from those without status. Those so called were tempted, like any of us, to turn the gift into a status".[58] Applying this to today's situation, we could say being a cleric does not give clerics some kind of social status that places them above others. This would create a gap between them and the laity. These are real risks for the pastoral ministry and we all need to guard against them.

On the desire to clericalise everyone, Pope Francis tells of his experience:

> When I served as a bishop in Buenos Aires, it happened on more than one occasion that good priests in conversation would say: 'I have a lay person in my parish who is worth his weight in gold!' And they made him seem like a "first class" layman. Then they asked me: 'What do you think about making him a deacon?' Here's where the problem lies: when a lay person is good at what they do, we immediately want to make them a deacon, we want to clericalise". (The Pope said this in response to a question regarding the fall in

---

58   Stanley Hauerwas, *Matthew*, Grand Rapids: Brazos Press, 2009, 161.

vocations, especially in places where there has been a reluctance to promote local vocations)..."Clericalism doesn't allow growth, it doesn't let the strength of baptism grow, it creates addictions that sometimes immerse entire populations in a powerful state of immaturity."[59]

The strength of Baptism and the role of the laity

This strength of Baptism deserves to be pondered for a moment. Another name for this is the theology of the laity since the laity are baptised. That is, what is the mission of the laity? What vision should inspire the laity? We will come to that presently.

To pose the question another way: this book is all about clericalism and one dimension of clericalism is that those ordained should not treat the laity as second class citizens in their church, nor infantilise them as Pope Francis is keen on saying, but encourage them to take up their rightful role. The question is: what is their rightful role? What is their mission?

Before answering that, let me refer to Pope Francis and how he demonstrated that he and the people are one in the church. On 12 March 2013, Pope Francis asked the people in St Peter's Square to give him their blessing – rather than the usual thing which is for him to give his blessing to them. In this he showed the priesthood of the faithful (a phrase we will explain shortly) as being important. The church is the people; they elect him as their servant to do a job.

---

[59] *Vatican Insider*. 28 January 2016. In a conversation between the Pope and Jesuits published by Jesuit periodical, *La Civiltà Cattolica*.

This then was a key moment, a magic moment, when he asked for the blessing of the people before giving his own, papal blessing. Many people throughout the world watched in amazement. Was this really happening? Had he given this much forethought? This was really a great way to make his point. I do not think this was spur of the moment thinking. I think it came from his many years of working close to people in Buenos Aires. It came from his total rejection of clericalism. This was simply his way of saying that all God's people are called to ask God to shower blessings and graces on each other. Actions speak louder than words.

If we enquire about the role of the laity, there are many documents to which we can refer, particularly those from Vatican II itself. The trouble is that not many people know about them and although they sound very impressive, nothing much has changed. Here are some of the most important documents coming from the Vatican Council. The documents are as follows in chronological order: The *Dogmatic Constitution on the Church* (*Lumen Gentium [LG]*), 21 November, 1964); *The Decree on the Apostolate of the Laity* (*Apostolicam Actuositatem [AA]*, 18 November, 1965); The *Pastoral Constitution on the Church in the Modern World*, (*Gaudium et Spes [GS]*, 7 December 1965); *Post-Synodal Apostolic Exhortation of John Paul II On the Vocation and The Mission of the Lay Faithful in the Church and In the World* (*Christifideles Laici* [LC], 30 December 1988).

These documents have many encouraging and inspirational sentences and perspectives of the role of the laity or – to use another term – the "theology of the laity". Unfortunately, there are also some other sentences that create a problem for an inclusive, contemporary theology for all members of the church. There are always problems in documents like these as the writers try to keep both ends of the continuum happy, both the progressives and conservatives. However there are many positive elements that can help us understand the role of the laity, in this place, and at this time. There are also some negative things that need to be faced.

Positive inclusive vision

Let us start with some positive aspects. There are some compelling and inspiring passages which speak about the People of God in an inclusive and new way and provide us with an inspirational vision of God's community very different to the hierarchical one. Chapter II of LG on *The People of God* and Chapter V, *On the Call of the Whole Church to Holiness*, has two such examples. Here, the terms "followers of Christ", "faithful of Christ" and "People of God" are inclusive terms frequently used which stress community. Points made in these passages apply to all in the Church. *The Decree on the Missionary Activity of the Church* (*Ad Gentes*) also has an inclusive introduction to the history of salvation speaking about "men" (meaning men and women) and "human beings". Salvation and mission is spoken of in terms of "human beings". This is said in contradistinction to *AA* which straight away utilises hierarchical language without any grand inclusive vision.

LG #40 also has an inclusive statement that reads as follows: "Thus it is evident to everyone that all the faithful of Christ of whatever rank or status are called to the fullness of the Christian life and to the perfection of charity." *GS* also has some striking passages. #1 sets the broad picture of humankind and the mission of the followers of Christ which is so inspiring. The key words here are "followers of Christ", "community", "kingdom of their Father" and "Holy Spirit". With the term "seeking the kingdom" (LG #31), the biblical image recalls the vastness of the missionary project which often goes beyond the confines of the visible church.

The divine energy

In AA #1, the point is made about the laity being aware of their role. It refers to "the unmistakeable work of the Holy Spirit in making the laity even more conscious of their responsibilities". *GS* also stresses the work of the Holy Spirit (called "pneumatology" in theology) in #1-3. In #1, it describes mission concisely: "United in Christ, they are led by the Holy Spirit in their journey to the Kingdom of their Father and they have welcomed the news of salvation which is meant for every man (and women!)".

The Vatican II documents draw attention to the emphasis on the Holy Spirit in the consciousness of the laity concerning their role. The basis of this is found in the Gospels, especially Luke. Everything that Jesus does, all his major moves, are preceded by the prompting of the Spirit. Let us take a sidestep for the moment and refresh our minds on the biblical source (Luke) of the inspiration of the Holy Spirit.

We can mention a few instances that show how complete this guidance of the Holy Spirit is in the life and mission of a number of people at the beginning of Luke's Gospel and in the life of Jesus. It can serve as a template for the laity and the ordained in the church today. If this is taken seriously by all, then it will mitigate the negative side of clericalism because we will all acknowledge the valid working of the Spirit in others in the church. Annabel's fury at her parish priest appointing a man to represent women at the diocesan level (see Case 5) is perhaps an example of failing to acknowledge the working of the Spirit in others.

Luke first of all speaks about John the Baptist, Mary, Simeon, Zachariah and Elizabeth. These are the instances: even from his mother's womb, he (John the Baptist) will be filled with the Holy Spirit (1:15); the Holy Spirit will come upon you (referring to Mary at the annunciation (1:35); now Elizabeth was filled with the Holy Spirit at the visitation (1:41); John the Baptist's father Zachariah was filled with the Holy Spirit (1:67); meanwhile the child grew up and his spirit matured (John the Baptist, a kind of refrain for Luke 1:80); And the Holy Spirit rested on him ... Simeon (2:25); it had been revealed to him by the Holy Spirit (discernment, 2:26); Prompted by the Spirit he came to the temple (2:27).

Luke moves on to Jesus and his mission and how every turn it took was inspired by the Holy Spirit. Filled with the Holy Spirit, Jesus left the Jordan and was led by the Spirit through the wilderness (temptation in the desert, 4:1); Jesus, with the power of the Spirit in him, returned to Galilee (driving force, 4:14); the Spirit of the Lord has been given to me ... (4:18); It was then that filled with the Holy Spirit he said ... (good news to the simple, 10:21); the Father gives the Holy Spirit to those who ask (11:13); the Holy Spirit will teach you what to say (12:12); a reference to power and what he promised you (24:49). And then there is the whole book called the Acts of the Apostles which continues Luke's message of the centrality of the Spirit to the Christian mission.

Integrated approach

Let us go back to the documents now. A little bit further on, AA #4 shows an integrated ideal of life, "for neither family concerns nor other secular affairs should be excluded from their religious program for life". #5 of the same document emphasises the inclusive aspect again: "It is the task of *the whole Church* to labour vigorously so that men (and women) may become capable of constructing the temporal order rightly and directing it to God through Christ". GS #3 tries to see the human person as one integrated person, body and soul. Other paragraphs in GS mention values like seeing human beings as made in God's image, the dignity of the human mind; truth and wisdom; respect for others, the excellence of liberty. #39 presents us with a wholistic view of creation, of the world. The world will be transformed it says. Therefore we should see all creation as a whole to be redeemed in some way. (This shows the inadequacies of the binary terms *"secular* or *religious",* or *"sacred* and *profane").* However, we must distinguish between earthly progress and God's kingdom. The first can serve the second. Finally, #43 tries to include the faithful/lay persons in the mission of the church: they have an active role to play in the whole church.

Examining the documents

Now for a closer look at some issues. The view seen above portrays a wholistic view of salvation, the people of God and mission. It does this by the language is uses and the inclusive, wholistic images it employs. But there is also another thread in the documents which is characterised by either/or language and concerns of the hierarchy.

We must bear in mind that the texts have a particular nature, that is, they are written by several people and need to satisfy right-wing and left-wing thinking. They are largely compromise texts. The documents were drafted by members of committees composed of Vatican officials, bishops and theologians which represented a wide range of theological opinion. These in turn may have relied on expert theologians who were available, and then discussed and amended drafts, depending on what the Theological Commission and individual bishops said about them. This process took months. When this process had been completed and many amendments had been incorporated into the text, the document was ready for a final vote by the full council of bishops. In order to satisfy all the objections and suggested amendments, and to ensure that the final vote was close to unanimous, the final document was a compromise in the sense that it sought to accommodate many and diverse points of view and sometimes almost contradictory viewpoints.

Definition of laity

The first issue is perhaps the definition of the word "laity". In LG #31, there is a brave attempt to define the laity in positive terms (all the faithful) but it too carries the negative side of "not being those in holy orders or religious". They live in the world, that is, in each and in all of the secular and professional occupations. In LG #10, the People of God include everyone baptised. This section is excellent for emphasising the commonalities. In the last few sentences of LG #10, the authors cannot help themselves and the text lapses into the distinction of the laity as those who do *not* share the ministerial priesthood. The difference between that and the common priesthood is left vague with the words, "In essence and not only in degree". Then the words, *power, rules, in essence*, indicate the clerical emphasis. The "in essence" is an allusion to the "ontological change" discussed above which fuels clerical attitudes.

One way of seeing the laity in the contemporary church is in terms of community/ministries rather than laity/clergy. This would require quite a change in the terminology we use when talking about people in the church. Language is extremely important when we discuss church understandings (called "ecclesiology" in theology) as language conveys assumptions, concepts, prejudices, points of view and sometimes entire philosophies of life. Therefore talking in terms of community/ministries has some pre-suppositions which need to be explained.

It is also interesting to note the use of the word "faithful" and "lay faithful". Actually, "the faithful" is used in some rare places meaning all the members of the church, but more normally it means the laity. Why should they be called the "faithful"? Who are the non-faithful or infidels in the church? The clergy? Obviously not. Moreover, the reference to the laity as "the faithful" has a paternalistic ring to it like referring to the laity as those who "pray, pay and obey". That era is over.

In reality, we should seldom speak about the laity and clergy and far more about the community and the ministries required in the service of the community and the mission of the community. That would begin to change the language and that would be a game changer.

You Speak, We Listen

Q: How would you explain to a Muslim friend who are the "laity" in your church?

Try to avoid negative language.

Q: Are there any religions where there are no clergy?

Dualism

Another fancy word for either/or is "dichotomy". It means dividing things into two parts, an either/or approach. This is also called the binary approach or a dualistic approach. A thing is either this or that. It has only two possibilities. It is either black or white, not grey. But what about a statement being partially true and partially untrue? It is not "true" and also not "false" but somewhere in between? This is a different way of thinking. Needless to say, the Catholic Church has always tended to adopt the dualistic approach: it is true or false. Hence the sad history of reformers who were persecuted by some enthusiastic hierarchs who labelled them as heretics because what they believed was "false".

But let us return to the documents. One of the issues that strikes one immediately is the dualism which is apparent in the frequent use of dichotomies in the text. Issues are often painted as either/or. People are either in the world or in the Church (AA #2). Priests are in the church and lay people in the world. Others are engaged in spiritual or temporal matters. One has a lay or priestly spirituality (AA #29). One is either engaged in temporal things or eternal ones. Lay people lead a secular life while priests live a sacred one. One either has a vocation (priesthood and religious life) or one does not. One is either a member of the hierarchy or lay.

What is wrong with this dualism? It is not the way most people live or experience their lives. For most people, I would maintain, life is an integrated experience where it is not that easy to say that this or that event, person, action or emotion, is secular or sacred. It comes down to the presence of God's grace which is "everywhere and everywhen". This was a point the great German theologian of Vatican II, Karl Rahner, spoke of and emphasised at the council. Most of life is fairly messy with good and evil often intertwined. It is not easy to judge that in a particular situation, God's grace is totally absent or totally present. Given that, it is simplistic to speak of a person engaged "in the world" and another one as engaged "in the church". It is not that simple to judge that this action is promoting the Kingdom of God and that other action is not.

We find this statement in LG #31, "But the laity, by their very vocation, seek the kingdom of God by engaging in temporal affairs". I would say in temporal and spiritual affairs, or better, seek the kingdom of God everywhere and everywhen. In all the documents, there is a persistent effort to box the laity into temporal affairs which, by implication, says: leave the spiritual affairs to us (clergy). That won't do. That is a clerical and dualistic outlook. None of that is found in the gospels. Jesus invites all to be involved in spiritual matters; spiritual enrichment and insights are offered to all.

We also read in LG #31 that "the layman is closely involved in temporal affairs of every sort". I would say that many priests I know are also involved in temporal affairs of every sort! We are dealing with a certain and definite clerical mindset in these passages. We must break out of this fixed view, this mould. It does not correspond to reality.

From a legal perspective, e.g. Canon Law, it is possible to say that this person is signed up to the church and hence "clergy" and that someone else is signed up to an institution which has nothing to do with religion and hence "secular".

But this is a legal approach. We are interested in investigating a theological and pastoral approach.

Dualism also conspires with compartmentalisation which desires to place everyone in a box and keep them there. The Roman bureaucracy is particularly given to seeing people in a particular place in the hierarchical church and hence in a box. This makes for tidy order and control. Canon law is invoked to determine which box the person is in and what their rights and obligations are.

You Speak, We Listen

Q: Have you ever felt this tension between being "in the world" or "in the church"?

Inclusive spirituality

Once one buys into dualism, there is the problem of trying to distinguish different kinds of spirituality for the boxes that have been created. Instead of constantly trying to fix different spirituality labels on people, the emphasis should be on what is the common basis for all the baptised.

AA #4, for example, is full of pious directions of following Christ and the poor which should equally apply to all people, all priests, all Christians. I find it paternalistic in tone. There should be more in the documents applicable to all members in the church and less on what separates. That would not sit well with the clericalism that underlies the many distinctions. This applies to AA # 29 which also stresses differences rather than commonalities. Emphasising the spiritual resources available to Christians by Baptism and the sacraments makes it possible to share the impressive, inclusive view that a theologian like E. Hahnenberg has of the Christian calling.[60]

In focusing on different spiritualities for people in different boxes, there was always the temptation to overlook the basic commonalities and virtues which all Christians should practise. Let me give an example: in the light of the clerical sexual abuse history, perhaps we, i.e. all members of the church, should concentrate more on basic common values like telling the truth, honesty, chastity, humility, service, respect for others, human equality, and less on hierarchy and privilege (clericalism). We find this in GS #4 and onwards.

Clericalism and role of priests

Clericalism is consistent with an attitude of wanting to compartmentalise everyone and keep people in their (inferior) place. Hence the extraordinary and paranoid *Instruction on Certain Questions Regarding the Collaboration of the Non-Ordained Faithful in the Sacred Ministry of Priests (1997)* in which the fear of some clergy that lay people would do them out of job is apparent. It was a certain misguided theology of priesthood, vocation and clericalism that created this demeaning document. Clericalism and a focus on hierarchy can distort the bigger picture. This narrow focus is captured by Cardinal Siri who during the discussion of *AA* (according to Yves Congar), thought only one thing was important to say and that was: the laity must submit to the hierarchy.[61] Such was his impoverished theology of the laity. No one will argue against the need of some hierarchy in human institutions but

---

60   Edward P. Hahnenberg, *Awakening vocation: A theology of Christian Call*. Collegeville: Liturgical Press, 2010.....
61   Yves Congar, *My Journal of the Council*, Adelaide: ATF, 2012, 391.

there has been a gross over-emphasis on it in the Catholic Church for many centuries, resulting in a skewered vision of the church (ecclesiology).

Regarding the particular role of priests, it is obvious that, given the history of the priesthood (related by Schillebeeckx[62] and others), their particular role has changed over the centuries. If the core elements of priesthood are proclaiming the gospel, administering the sacraments and spiritual leadership, there are many ways these can be done and many ways of collaboration with other members of the church. If, however, the way the role of the priest as currently exercised is seen as unchangeable and a power game, it will also be seen as the line in the sand to lay ambition. This approach gives expression to the document mentioned above entitled, *Instruction on Certain Questions Regarding the Collaboration of the Non-Ordained Faithful in the Sacred Ministry of Priests (1997)* which is filled with clerical paranoia. A narrow focus on control and power over people is a far cry from the expansive and inspiring vision of community/ministries and mission.

The vision of the document *Ad Gentes* could serve as the basis for a theology for all members of the church. In the opening paragraphs, although the role of the Apostles is clearly stated, nevertheless, it is the "Church" which is summoned with special urgency to save and renew every creature. The document also acknowledges the work done so far "through the noble energy of the whole Church". It is the "people of God" (everyone) who must spread the kingdom of God. This is a very inclusive vision of what is expected of all

---

[62] E. Schillebeeckx, *The Church with a Human Face: a new and expanded theology of ministry*. New York: Crossroad, 1985.

members. It makes the laity co-responsible with the ordained for the mission.

If the Church is missionary by nature, it means that all its members must be missionary orientated. That is the opposite of members being passive and seeing Church attendance once a week as their only obligation. The theology of mission takes its origin in the Trinity and then is worked out through the ministry of Christ. Members continue this ministry by following the same road Christ took: one of poverty and obedience, of service and self-sacrifice to the death – a death from which he came forth a victor in the Resurrection.

You Speak, We Listen

Q: How did you see the role of the priest when growing up? How do you see it now?

Laity as priest, prophet and king

For the first three centuries, all followers of Jesus Christ saw each other as equals although people had various roles in the Christian church, e.g. apostles, preachers, teachers, healers, speakers in tongues, etc. They all wore the dress of the day. You could not identify their role by their dress. Baptism was the sacrament that made them equal to other Christians. They formed the discipleship or community of equals. They were not interested in hierarchy or their status among other Christians. These statements are generalisations to some extent as communities developed along their own lines.

Today, a bishop like the Australian Vincent Long has said he wants us to see church as a community of equals. We must emphasise what we have in common. No-one should enjoying privileges above others in the church. This approach has its obligations too. The laity must now be prepared to assume responsibilities in the church and not leave everything to the parish priest or religious. It is their church as much as the priests. Cardinal Martini called this the co-responsibility of the laity. The laity have been used to sitting back and letting the priest do everything. Their role was to "pray, pay and obey". This must change. In a community of equals, we must all pull our weight.

Not surprisingly, Pope Francis has stressed this new emphasis on the role of the laity.[63] He has strikingly called for continued development of the role of lay people in the Catholic Church, saying they cannot be considered "'second class' members" after priests and religious but instead participate in Christ's priestly role through their own work in the world. He has also stated that the Second Vatican Council "brought, among its many fruits, a new way of looking at the vocation and the mission of lay people in the church and in the world".

Reflecting particularly on the conciliar constitutions LG and GS, Francis says those documents state that lay people "participate, in their own way, in the priestly, prophetic and royal function of Christ himself". What does this mean? Through words and actions, we can all proclaim the Good News and in doing so we are exercising our prophetic role. We decry injustice and proclaim justice, according to the gospels. It is what is known as the common (or universal) priesthood of all. This piece of theology has been largely sidelined in Catholicism, especially after the Reformation. This hesitation is seen in the recent (2016) document, *The Gift of the Priestly Vocation*, which has chosen to avoid even using the phrase, "common priesthood of all believers".

In offering our life, our every action, all our efforts, as a sacrifice to God, we are exercising our priestly role. We are offering a sacrifice, our life. A priest also connects this world with the transcendent (the spiritual world). We too

---

63   The references that follow come from an article by Joshua J. McElwee. Cf in *National Catholic Reporter*.

can do this. In our good actions, we act as a connecting point between God and others which is another way to see our priestly role. We let God's grace work through us and this can be an encouragement to others.

Finally, our role as king can be tricky. We do not want to emphasise a king as conquering other nations and lording it over them. We reject that model. However, when we try to triumph over sin, when we control ourselves and conquer temptation, we play a kingly or royal role in conquering our weakness. Furthermore, when we think of Christ the King, we model ourselves on him, not a King in battle but as a servant King. Thus in seeing ourselves is a kingly role, we see our role as one of service not lording it over others. So the three traditional roles of prophet, priest and king can be a very comprehensive way of seeing the role of the laity. It is a big challenge. It is far removed from a seemingly passive role of one who only prays, pays and obeys.

You Speak, We Listen

Q: *Does this idea of the lay person as priest, prophet and king speak to you today? Explain why you agree or disagree.*

Q: *What has inspired you to live your Christian life in a better way?*

Case 5

Mad-made misogyny

One of the recurring aspects of clericalism is the way some clergy relate to women. I suppose given the way women were kept out of the seminaries and teaching theology, it is no wonder that it became a problem. Added to this was the way women were regarded outside the church, in society in general in the West, although things have changed, and are changing for the better. Given also that women make up more than fifty percent of most parishes, the problem has become the elephant in the room.

Rejection and discrimination

Here is the story of a mature-aged woman, Annabel, who has given much to the church, has thought long and hard about many life issues, and is dedicated to growth in the spiritual life but has experienced rejection in the church. She writes:

> A few years ago, I attended the Liturgical Ministry Formation training program in our Diocese. All participants were encouraged to attend all evenings up to and including the training night for acolytes. I did

this as, at the time, I was very interested in becoming an Adult Server and was told that this evening would assist the female adult server, as women cannot become acolytes.

When I attended this night, I realised that as acolytes the men were to further attend an evening at the Cathedral with the Bishop to be inducted as acolytes. The alternative for women adult servers, who will perform the same duties as the male acolytes, was the same as all other persons who received training i.e. readers, eucharistic ministers and minister to the sick, that they are given their certificate by the local parish priest. I cannot begin to express my feeling of rejection and discrimination as a female member of the Catholic Church.

This story reveals one of the major problems within the church, i.e. how we treat women. Given how women have slowly been acknowledged in society in general (at least in the western world, as they now have education opportunities and can follow a career), the church is still stuck in medieval times regarding the role of women. Perhaps it is not difficult to see why – the decisions-makers in the church are mainly elderly, celibate males. Their attitude towards women fits into the clerical culture of superiority and privilege.

Annabel speaks of feelings of discrimination and rejection which clericalism evokes. We have heard Pope Francis already on precisely this point: clericalism alienates members of the church and reinforces the belief that priests are superior to the laity. He is relentless:

> Of course, this isn't the first time that Pope Francis has spoken out against clericalism – in fact, it could easily

be considered one of the most frequently-repeated topics of his pontificate; most recently to a group of Jesuits, but he has also strongly condemned it in the Church in Latin America.[64]

There is no argument to indicate why women cannot be acolytes, and the absence of any rational argument points to further infantilisation of the laity. No argument is given because the cleric is superior to the rest. This attitude is so arrogant we can begin to identify with Annabel.

The fury of Annabel is echoed in this comment from Chloe:

> A pastor in our parish appointed a man (without consulting with any female parishioners) as our parish women's representative at the diocesan level.

Another story shows not only the prejudice against women in the church but the prejudice of ageism. Maria had been going to a parish for many years but when a new, conservative priest was appointed, things changed. She expressed her concern to the priest as she could see the parish sliding backwards into a pre-Vatican II church.

She writes as follows: "With growing concern for my parish, I approached the priest to find out what was going on. After a lengthy civil discussion, on my part, and a patronising response on his, I realised that it was pointless to continue 'as father knows best'". One rejection did not put her off although his clericalism was evident. She then recounts what happened next:

> Then an opportunity came up, or so I thought, to be appointed to the diocesan Deanery. The catch was that the parish priest had to sign and endorse the application. I made an appointment and took my application up to him. He laughed at me and told me I was too old, at 69 years. They only wanted young people he said, with new ideas. Enquiring at the diocesan level as to whether that was the actual case, I was told no, they wanted representatives from all age groups. What was really telling was that another woman, slightly younger and highly qualified, also applied but to no avail. The priest, in his wisdom, had decided that two males were more appropriate and so it continues.

You Speak, We Listen

Q: How are older people treated in the church, in your experience?

Q: Do younger people always have the new ideas?

Misogyny: some history

The struggle of women for their rightful place in the church continues. Many voices ask that women not only be made deacons but that they too be ordained. It seems part of the evolution of humankind and of women in particular. If one considers the trajectory of women in the church in the last millennium, we see the following. Women were not allowed on the sanctuary (except to do the flowers), they had to wear a veil on their head in church, they were not allowed to do the readings at Mass, they (girls) were not allowed to be altar girls, they were not made deacons, they were not allowed to be acolytes, they were not allowed to be ordained. To go back to Bishop Centellas, the bishop of Potosi in Bolivia, and the Synod for the Amazon and contemporary times: Bishop Centellas, during a synod news briefing on 23 October, told reporters that while women are "the majority" in the church, "their participation in the organisation and decisions in the life and mission of the church is very little." He continued: "I think that if we do not change structures, if we do not change our way of organising ourselves, that will not change".

Slowly, women were permitted to be altar girls, walk in the sanctuary, do the Mass readings, be made senior servers, be pastoral assistants (almost parish priests), run sacramental programs, teach in seminaries, be made chancellors of dioceses. Who doubts that the trajectory will stop there? Who doubts that they will be pastors one day as they are in some Christian churches today without the heavens falling in?

Women and Vatican II

Vatican II was a watershed in Catholicism. We might well ask what sort of picture did they paint of women in the church? None of the Vatican II documents above mentions the ordination of women but *CL* (a post-conciliar document) has an extraordinary number of sentences about Christian women. It comes across as if the authors (the bishops) have a guilty conscience about the treatment of Christian women in the Catholic Church. The denial of ordination for women is defended at length with the "complementarity" argument which many reject as spurious (men and women complement each other but have different roles). No mention is made of the biblical study into whether the Bible is for or against the ordination of women that Pope Paul VI instigated. (It found that the evidence is neither for nor against the ordination of women.) These sentences from *CL* often give a good basis for concluding that women should be ordained, yet the opposite is stated. So the unsatisfactory theology on the laity continues to include this unsatisfactory theology of the refusal to ordain women.

On this issue, the official Catholic position presents a theology and an anthropology (understanding of humankind) which are unconvincing. Perhaps one should apply the "hermeneutics of suspicion" (looking for other reasons) and look at the sociology of power at play. The Catholic Church never seems to speak of power when talking about itself; it is the elephant in the room. Yet if the church is human (and it is), power must be a force with which one must reckon. In the Catholic hierarchy, one has a group of celibate, ageing males who have all the power and are unwilling to share this with females. It comes down to power play. Could this theory be correct? There are parallels of this kind of power play in the defence forces, business, academic and political worlds. It is a theory that could be valid.

Some women have said they would not like to be pastors now, while this critical model of priesthood prevails. They look for a change in the way pastors function before they would accept the role. Part of the change would be from priest to pastor. From the cultic high priest model to the servant-pastor model.

In Australia, in more recent times, the ACBC took on a project on women in the church which resulted in a publication called *Woman and Man: One in Christ Jesus*, 1999. Now twenty years later, they have re-visited the topic and produced another book, *Still Listening to the Spirit: Woman and Man 20 Years On* (2019). The comment of the authors is that "There is unfinished business from the action commitments made by the bishops in 2000". Others might say nothing much has changed. Sandie Cornish, a co-author of the second publication, commented that many of the major themes considered in *Woman and Man: One in Christ Jesus* "remain live and contentious... While there have been advances in some areas, little seems to have changed in others, and in some matters, things seem to have gone backwards," she wrote.[65] So change seems to be very slow in coming, if at all. (Perhaps this shows again that the underlying issue of clericalism must be addressed.)

---

65   CathNews,https://cathnews.com/cathnews/36752-promoting-women-in-the-church-unfinished-business.accessed 29 November 2019.

Catalysts for Renewal (Australia), in their submission to the ACBC regarding the 2020 Plenary Council, stated very clearly what their expectations were regarding women. Let me quote them in full:

> We believe the Catholic Church must recognise the essential role of women in every area of church life – in leadership, in ministry and in governance.
>
> Since women fill more roles than men in Catholic parishes, schools, hospitals, aged care and charitable organisations, we call on church leaders to take steps to have women in all levels of decision-making, including senior leadership positions.
>
> We believe that the Holy Spirit is asking that women today are given their rightful, complementary and equal place at all levels. Women should, where theologically, formationally and/or professionally competent, be appointed as part of decision-makers and leaders at every level of the structure and governance of the church, in theological colleges, seminaries, diocesan structures and parishes.[66]

You Speak, We Listen

Q: Do you agree that the church is "stuck in medieval times" regarding the treatment of women?

Q: What action would you take to remedy this situation?

---

66 Catalysts For Renewal Incorporated, submission to the Plenary Council 2020, The Future of the Catholic Church in Australia. February 2019. http://catalystforrenewal.org.au

> Q: Describe how your parish would change if a leading woman became chair of the parish council and the parish priest had no right of veto.
>
> Q: Say what you agree with, or disagree with, in the statement from the Catalysts for Renewal above.

Women priests?

In the small-group meetings that have taken place in view of the Plenary Council in Australia, it is clear that people want to talk about the ordination of women and are not put off by the previous ban on the topic by Pope John Paul II. There has been a strong voice from those who want women priests as well as a strong opposition. To others it seems common sense to expand the pool of people who feel the call to priesthood to include women. At a meeting of *Concerned Catholics* in Canberra, a former journalist, Mark Metherell, reported the following:

> The former NSW Premier, Kristina Keneally, spoke about the church's failure to address reality. She recalled being at Mass where the priest made an appeal for vocations. In the congregation, she observed two former, now married, priests and four women she knew to have theological degrees.[67]

Those who oppose women priests rely pretty heavily on saying that the tradition does not allow for them, that it would be against the authentic teaching of the Catholic Church, and that Jesus chose only men to be his apostles. They also say a

---

67 Mark Metherell, "The Need for Catholic Church Reform", *Concerned Catholics*, 15 May 2017.

female cannot represent Jesus who was a male. This is the position that Pope Francis and previous popes have taken.

On the other hand, the argument for ordained women has many elements: the need for inclusivity and gender equality (Galatians 3:26-29); the present ban is a social construct and can be changed; it is outright discrimination to exclude women; it would allow women into the power structure of the church (and would have avoided the cover-ups of child sexual abuse in the church); it would supplement the clergy shortage; it would realign the church with the role of women in society today (in western countries).

Let us first go back to the Early Church. In the gospels, a number of women followed Jesus from the first days of his mission (Luke 8:2). They came from Galilee in the first instance and followed him to Judea and through Samaria. They ministered to him and looked after his daily needs. They were there in Jerusalem at this trial and crucifixion. They did not abandon him at his trial and crucifixion, unlike the apostles who fled in fear. They stood by him to the end. After his death, it was a woman, Mary Magdalene, who was the first to be a witness to the resurrection. The women as a group became the first preachers of the resurrection (Luke 24:9).

Paul never saw Jesus in the flesh and was not a witness to the resurrection (a criterion for being an apostle), but considered himself an apostle. Consider Mary Magdalene: she followed Jesus from the earliest day, ministered to him, went to Jerusalem and stood by Jesus on Golgotha and then was the first witness to the resurrection ahead of Peter (Mark 16:9-10). Did she not have all the qualifications for being an apostle? Whatever happened to her in the early church? After the resurrection, we hear very little about Mary of Magdala except in extracanonical literature such as the Gospel of Thomas and the Gospel of Mary.

Women were prominent in the first years of the church after the resurrection. Paul mentions women in leadership roles in Romans 16:1-15. There was Phoebe, a deacon of the church, Prisca and Aquila, who Paul says ran a house church and "are my fellow workers in Christ Jesus who risked death to save my life". Mary who "worked so hard for you", and Tryphena, Tryphosa, Junias Julia, Nereus' sister. And possibly others as it is not always clear if the names are male or female.

There are a number of theories as to why women disappeared from leadership roles so soon after the resurrection. The one that makes most sense to me is that the male leaders in the church did not want the Christian church to appear to be a church of "women and children". They wanted to be like the other religions and society where men ruled the roost, so they got rid of female leadership.

Mary Magdalene

One of the signs of misogyny in the church is the legend around Mary Magdalene. In the gospels it says she was possessed of seven demons which Gregory the Great (6th century) and others, thought meant grave sinfulness, and in particular, that she was a forgiven prostitute. Today the "seven demons" are thought to mean a severe illness, the "seven" indicating the severity of the sickness. (The Eastern Church has never viewed her as a prostitute but as the "Apostle of the Apostles"). This is just one example of the misogyny that crept into the church and remained ever since. In spite of this, great women like Hildegard of Bingen, Clare of Assisi, Joan of Arc, Theresa of Avila, Catherine of Siena, Therese

Mad-made misogyny

of Lisieux, Theresa of Calcutta, to name a few, have shown that there were great women leaders in spite of misogyny. Although some abbesses in church history had great power in the church, the overall culture of misogyny continued to this day. One has only to think of St Mary McKillop and her struggles with local bishops to confirm that opinion and the stories mentioned above.

With the Enlightenment and modern times, human rights have come to the fore and with it the rights and role of women in society have slowly been recognised but not in the church which is stuck in the past and in its clericalism. Pope Benedict realised this and on a few occasions said women should have decision-making authority in the church but was unable to translate that into practice. Pope Francis has in fact taken some action on this matter.

Misogyny has been part of the culture of clericalism. Women have been looked down upon and often treated as slaves. The role of women religious looking after seminarians is one manifestation of that. The Report of the Plenary Council expresses this frustration and misogyny very aptly:

> It is critical to open up opportunities for women priests, deacons and acolytes, not simply use them as support staff – as readers, catechists, flower arrangers, vestment launderers and church cleaners, while telling them patronisingly how valuable they are.[68]

In society in general, these behaviours are still present although changing. Sometimes in groups of mixed people, the men are the only ones who count. The opinions of women are not sought. Some roles are only for men.

---

68 *Listen to what the Spirit is saying*, op. cit., p. 81.

This translates into the church as well. Recently, to my surprise, I was told of how a local parish needed someone with a financial background for volunteer parish work. The chair of the council tapped a certain male parishioner on the shoulder and suggested he was the right person. The man replied that he did not have the experience in that area but his wife did. The chair replied that they were looking for a man! The prejudice continues.

The ordination of women is bound to come sooner or later. Part of the tradition of the Catholic Church is to change. Retired Bishop Cullinane expresses it this way:

> But the Catholic tradition is about being faithful in an ever changing world. Historically, the Church has always adapted to changing social and cultural conditions, in order to carry out its unchanging mission. Not to adapt is to not be faithful to that tradition or to that mission.[69]

So although banned for the present, I would expect the culture in the church regarding women to change. After all, as Cardinal Martini, the former archbishop of Milan, has pointed out: the Catholic Church is about two hundred years behind the times! [70]

It has a lot of catching up to do! As a German archbishop diplomatically opined many years ago when asked about women priests: the trajectory of the role of women in the church has changed and is only going in one direction.

---

69 Cullinane, op. cit.
70 Cardinal Carlo Maria Martini in his last interview in *Corriere della Sera*, August 2012.

You Speak, We Listen

Q: What do you think of the argument above for and against women's ordination?

Q: What benefits would they bring to the ordained ministry?

Q: Why do some women not support the present model of priesthood?

Do something near you

Before getting down to concrete proposals to eradicate clericalism, let us make a few general comments that feed into our proposals. Any attempt to bring about change is going to be long and hard. We know this from our human experience.

Witness the difficulties with banks, police forces, hospitals and others in trying to bring about change. The church is no different in this respect. We need to be warned of what lies ahead.

Progress slow: four warnings

In the process of change and moving forward, we must expect change to be slow and unsure. Two authors[71] warn us that in an ever changing world, churches and their leadership (ordained and lay, men and women) must accept and work with some problems.

> **WARNING: WORK IN PROGRESS. YOU MAY EXPERIENCE DELAYS**
> 1) Ambiguity, 2) Disruptive Change, 3) Risk, and 4) Modern Communication Systems.

---

[71] Michael Anderson and Miranda Jefferson, *Transforming Organizations: Engaging the 4Cs for powerful organizational learning and change.* London: Bloomsbury Business, 2019.

These four factors apply to the Catholic Church right now. What exactly will change is not that clear and very *ambiguous*. The Pope comes out with a new document and some misinterpret what he is saying. Those with binary thinking cannot tolerate grey areas. Bishops seem to contradict each other and leave many with doubts and ambiguity.

The NCR has picked up on this point of ambiguity or confusion: "The word 'confusion' is often applied by those who find unsettling Francis' more pastoral approach compared to recent papacies. His language and even his daily routine follow his clear intent to remove the stench of royalty and privilege from the world of Catholic leadership."[72]

However, the editorial in NCR also says that this confusion could be a blessing in disguise: "If a little confusion exists, maybe it is a blessing, leading, if not to absolute answers, then, far more important, to correct questions. If the original Twelve who encountered the living Christ are any example, we can take serious consolation. They are the best indicators that faith is not a matter of certainty and that confusion can be a path that sends us deeper into the mystery".

The huge resistance to Pope Francis, especially from the USA, and many bishops throughout the world, adds the disruptive element to attempts at change. Some groups in the church want to revive practices of the past, like saying Mass in Latin and memorising the catechism. Would having married and celibate pastors cause more disruption? Some want ecumenical connections severed or interfaith dialogue

---

72 "Editorial: If a little Catholic confusion exists, maybe it is a blessing" *NCR*, 6 December, 2019. Also see Michael Sean Winters, "Pope Francis' fourth Anniversary: will reforms work?" *NCR,* March 2017. Michael Sean Winters is NCR Washington columnist and a visiting fellow at The Catholic University of America's Institute for Policy Research and Catholic Studies.

with Muslims banned. Pope Francis has attracted much personal criticism for what he says and has disrupted many comfortable lives: "Francis, in his critique of an economy that 'kills' or in his absolute condemnation of the possession of nuclear weapons, as well as his severe criticism of the excesses of the clerical culture, has certainly afflicted the comfortable on many levels and in more than a few corridors of power".[73]

The risk of further schisms is always there, whether it is over the ordination of women, or bishops and priest losing some of their power, or the role of the laity, or over homosexuality. One priest wanted to forbid an ecumenical service with the Uniting Church lest all the Catholics in his parish (yes, his parish!) became Uniting Church members. Overall, we live with risks all the time.

The challenge of working in a digital world with quite different patterns of communication is huge. People cannot be banned from communicating with themselves, and secrecy is undermined by an email to hundreds of people. Hierarchy and secrecy (two elements in clericalism) is correct in seeing internet and emails as a threat to secrecy and hierarchy. The day of the supremacy of the church bulletin is over, as is the diocesan propaganda newspaper featuring the bishop on every other page. Many independent church newspapers and websites have exposed the sexual abuse scandals. The church must adapt to the internet, mobile phones, twitter, Facebook, instagram and all the rest.

---

[73] Ibid.

You Speak, We Listen

Q: *Can you tell the group how you have experienced these four elements of the warning?*

Conclusions

What are the conclusions we can come to regarding clericalism? The sexual child abuse scandal has shaken the church and highlighted the need for reform. But not all bishops are convinced about the need for reform; in fact, some do not seem to have realised the seriousness of the situation. They just do not "get it" as many parishioners say.

Clericalism has many facets to its nature. There is a convincing argument to show it has contributed to the sexual abuse scandal. It has been identified as a major issue in the Catholic Church today by Pope Benedict and Pope Francis. The latter has spoken tirelessly about it in the face of resistance from many bishops and cardinals, especially in the USA. The idea that priests are somehow superior to others in the church is supported by a large section of the church. Just how big we don't know.

If there is to be any significant reform in the attempt to get rid of clericalism, the changes must be structural and related to power in the church. Changes at the edges of church life will do nothing to reform the church. Bishops and priest have too much power at the moment. Their power must be reduced as was stated by German bishops in the Introduction to this book. They need to be made accountable, transparent and responsible. The laity must share the power at the local and diocesan levels. Synods must include the laity. The role of the pastor must be reduced and focused on spirituality and the laity must be allowed (and they must be willing!) to share the running of the church. The Catalysts for Renewal summed it up accurately when they said: "Power in the church should be exercised with grace and humility and in the interests of the church and its people. Presently, power is inextricably bound to ordination. This nexus should be broken, in our opinion."[74]

Worldwide, the Vatican must continue to de-centralise the church and change the curia who have assumed to run the church instead of serving the church.

The human weaknesses in the church will continue and the laity must be held accountable and not allowed to fall into the clerical model we know today.

Before we consider a more formal assembly of things to do to eradicate clericalism, we can report two different sources of wisdom.

First, an article by Bigelow in which she talks about her parish, St Mary's, and how they promoted a culture of inclusiveness to overcome clericalism. At St Mary's, her parish, "a culture of inclusive collaboration gradually took root as laypeople and priests joined together to leverage the Church's institutional power on behalf of the most marginalised members of the local community. Over time, they developed structures and practices to ensure that, no matter who the pastor happened to be, the laity would retain a guiding voice in the parish's mission." [75]

The key words here are "structures and practices".

In addition, they did not try to abolish the priesthood but rather set about the more painstaking work of "transforming

---

[74] Catalysts for Renewal, op.cit.
[75] Reynolds, op.cit.

the ecclesial structures that engender and sustain this diseased understanding of clerical supremacy".[76]

Secondly, what do online readers of an independent Catholic newspaper think about this issue? Bloggers were asked by *La Croix* to say in what ways clericalism could be eradicated. An initial response came up with a variety of ways, some of which we have already encountered in the above pages.

I will list them without trying to put them in order. One was to reduce the number of popes who become saints. This only increases clericalism. This came up more than once. Another was to get rid of the vestments, and mitres and other addenda. Better sermons and correcting the all masculine aspects of the liturgy like masculine pronouns and nouns in the readings. The promotion of the spiritual life of clergy was another. (When did your pastor last speak of his spiritual journey?) It is the church that makes priests not the other way around. Here was another: by focusing on the poor, sick and marginalised, ambition, power and self-interest will fall away (this is what Reynolds above is saying happened in her parish). We all are part of the church. There is a need to teach the ecclesiology of communion. The Christian life is not about success and power. We should return to our ministry from our Baptism. [77]

Do something

Having said all of the above, we can now come down to the nitty-gritty. Many will be waiting to know "what can I do"? Or "what can my parish do?" This is where we need self-starters,

---

76 Ibid.
77 *La Croix*, 23 September 2018.

but the Catholic Church is not noted for encouraging this in recent centuries.

The heading of this chapter, 'Do Something Near You',[78] is the name of a movement founded by Sandra Sully and John Dee in Australia to get people to volunteer to do something practical near them, instead of criticising and doing nothing. We can follow their example and transfer that thinking to the church. The laity (mostly) have got too used to sitting back and letting the ordained do all the work. Where we do have good lay leaders, they are often over-worked and end up suffering burn-out. Priests too can suffer burn-out (in fact the model operating in some dioceses now is a cyclic one that overworks the priests and then when they suffer burnout and resign, those left standing are asked to do yet more with more burnouts. This is a life-threatening model.)

John Paul II, moreover, says that priests who have been actively involved in the ministry for a more or less lengthy period of time seem to be suffering today from an excessive loss of energy in their ever increasing pastoral activities. Likewise, faced with the difficulties of contemporary culture and society, they feel compelled to re-examine their way of life and their pastoral priorities, and they are more and more aware of their need for ongoing formation (*Pastores Dabo Vobis* #3). I would see this as the result of too much work and need for a re-conceptionalising of the role of the ordained; clericalism pushes us in the direction that the parish priest can do everything. No, he cannot.

The process of change will take a long time and require patience. Nevertheless, the Bolivian bishop already referred to above, acknowledged that the eradication of clericalism "is a very long process of a change of mentality". This change

---

78 https://dosomethingnearyou.com.au/#

will not happen just by ordaining women deacons or married men. He pointed to the crux of the matter: "I think the problem is that we have yet to understand what it means to be a church of communion, a synodal church", he said. "With the current structures, we won't go very far."

Changing the culture or mentality of a group is not easy or done quickly. We mentioned the four dangers above. Culture is something deeply engrained in a people and established over many years, as pointed out in the Introduction. In its broadest sense, culture is the total way of life of a group, tribe or nation. In a more restricted sense, it is the way a certain group of people behave in a given human activity. The police force, the banks, football clubs, netball associations all have their culture with respect to their activity. Changing that way of doing things is always a challenge.

An example that comes to mind is that of the police force in Australia. Because of complaints alleging that the police treated indigenous Australians poorly, different commissions have investigated to see if this were true. In particular it was noted that Aboriginal people who were sent to jail were often inclined to die in jail, often reported as suicide. The problem was deep and ongoing. So a royal commission (1987-1991) was set up to investigate. The report from the commission concluded that there were glaring deficiencies in the standard of care afforded to many of the deceased. The commission also made three hundred and thirty-three recommendations, but today, nearly twenty years later, the number of deaths have increased and many recommendations have not been implemented. Changing the culture which resulted in many deaths in custody has proved too difficult to achieve. The recommendations will have to be re-visited and reasons sought why the culture has not changed.

So too with clericalism in the church. Recommendations will be made, new ways of doing things will be suggested, and time will tell if the culture has changed.

Now we can move to the setting out of possible changes we can promote. We can look at the problems and solutions from a structural and educational and attitudinal viewpoint. All of these can run at the same time.

Structural and governance changes

These changes will need to be worked through at parish and diocesan levels. There are various ways of doing this. Parishioners can use both existing structures and new ones, like a group of parish or diocesan leaders. They might well be mainly lay people although the ideal is to have pastors working in the group.

Number 1. Selection/election of bishops

Regarding criteria, Peter Daly has spoken about this and so have many since Vatican II. Here small groups could make suggestions and forward them to reform groups, to the local bishop or the Pope. The criteria might include: a certain number of years in a parish; a record of working for the poor or less privileged in their community; an exemplified pastoral approach (as opposed to a juridical approach); a record of support in ecumenical and interfaith work; a habit of spiritual reading and updating their theology.

The election of bishops should also be done by all the faithful, lay and ordained. Mews reminds us that before the Council of Trent, bishops were chosen by "clergy and people".[79] This method should be re-introduced. This idea has not been entirely lost over the centuries. In Switzerland there was in recent times the case of the local diocese not accepting the conservative bishop that Rome wanted to impose. The issue was resolved in the bishop not taking up his post. Although bishops were chosen by all in the early centuries, since Trent the centralisation of Rome has continued apace. Today we still have the Pope as the one who decides who is to be bishop in a diocese. If he does not like the list of candidates that are presented to him by the bureaucracy, he can appoint someone else.

The more traditional route to becoming a bishop included a doctorate in Canon Law (the rules of the Catholic Church) which often gave bishops a juridical approach to problems rather than a pastoral. Let me illustrate with an example.

While I was in Chicago at the United Theological Union many years ago on Sabbatical, a group of us met for dinner one night. This was the late 1990s. A pastor from Canada told us about the first child sexual abuse case he heard of (this was a first for me too). He said the distraught parents of the victim went to see their bishop only to be told he couldn't see them and they had better get a lawyer. "But he is our pastor", they protested. "Sorry, see a lawyer." What a slap in the face to the parents! Many others too sadly could only think of lawyers and compensation rather than compassion. That is a direct result of a certain clerical mindset and culture of promoting those with a PhD in Canon Law.

---

79 Constant Mews, in Berise Heasly, *Call No One Father*, Melbourne: Coventry Press, 14.

Number 2. Limit number of canonised popes

The number of popes or clergy in general who are made saints should be limited. The impression currently given is that saints come from the clerical category rather than the laity.

Number 3. Limit hierarchs

The number of the hierarchy could be limited too. There should be one category of bishops (no archbishops) and no cardinals, monsignori, archdeacons or any other category. Having many categories or steps up the ladder, seems to encourage career-climbers. Titles and careerism go together. There are those who join the clergy with a higher role as bishop, or cardinal, in view. Phyllis Zagano, an American academic and advocate of the ordination of women as deacons, sums it up accurately thus:

> ... Clericalism is real. Yes, I know clerical cronyism spills out from fancy restaurants, appears in box seats at sports events, and finds its way to Caribbean cruises and vacations. Over expensive dinners, or along with the beer and hot dogs, or between piña coladas, the players trade their chips and gather gossip. It has everything to do with careerism and nothing to do with ministry.[80]

Careerism has always been a part of clericalism and is antithetical to the role of pastor as servant.

---

80   Phyllis Zagano, "Just Catholic", *NCR*, 5 June 2016..

Number 4. The power structure in the Catholic Church needs reform

The power of the bishop and parish priest must be curtailed. Currently, the Pope appoints bishops and can fire them. Other bishops cannot interfere in a diocese, only the Pope. But the pope lives far away and there are many bishops in the world. The pope cannot possibly attend to all bishops.

A bishop can do what he wants to, because he only answers to the pope. If he was responsible to the episcopal conference too, his powers would be limited. No bishop wants another bishop to tell him what to do. We live with that situation. For example, each bishop wants his own newspaper or bulletin, so that he can control what goes into it and promote himself. Any suggestion of a national Catholic paper is rejected because each bishop wants his own. The result is no national, high standard paper, just each diocese has its own newspaper. (This situation has been partially countered by the many high standard independent online Catholic newspapers.)

A bishop should be accountable to a body of elders in the diocese who have the right to refuse the bishop certain actions.

A parish priest also has too much power. He should be answerable to a parish council or body of elders (elected by the parishioners), and to the bishop.

Number 5. Selection of those to be ordained

Other than the psychological and personality testing that is essential after all the sexual abuse scandal, for those preparing for ordination, the right motivation seems important. Personal skills in communicating with others, a deep spiritual life, humility, and love of the gospels, an understanding of the use and abuse of power (all this is aimed at those who might be career seekers aiming at becoming a bishop and then an archbishop and then a cardinal - even becoming Pope!).

Candidates could be chosen from existing lay men and women who have proved themselves in parish work. We all know many such loyal parishioners. Older people could be prepared.

Number 6. Ordination preparation

It is clear that traditional seminary training promotes clericalism. We need to find new ways of preparing candidates for ordination. Seminaries were introduced after Trent to help bishops train people for ordination as opposed to bishops ordaining good people without any education and preparation, to stand in front of the congregation and try to read the prayers in Latin. We have come a long way from that. Seminaries have long and complicated curriculums involving philosophy and theology and much else. We have discussed a new curriculum for the preparation of ordination candidates. The details of this argument have been worked out above in Case 2.

Number 7. Promote the spiritual life

More needs to be done to promote the spiritual wellbeing of the clergy and laity. It should be obvious in a parish that the spiritual journey is more important than collecting money, building churches, running trivia nights or organising netball teams. Spiritual directors should be discussed and used. The spiritual journey of all of us should be openly discussed and preached about.

The images we use of God must not be used as a template for submissiveness of the laity. For example, God as seen as almighty, omnipotent and supreme must not be used as a tool leading to a culture of submission to the holy which can be used to support clericalism. This theology can be used as religious manipulation under the guise of the divine will.

Number 8. Promote women

This is not new at all. Many have suggested this. We suggest a women chair of the parish council. This is a good idea because it could change the tone and attitudes of parish councils. Currently, many councils are simply rubber stamps for the local parish priest. There have been some good guidelines in some dioceses but it seems to me the local parish priest has too much scope to do as he wishes. This suggestion of having a woman in charge needs further examination. Details need to be worked out. If she has a veto on any motion, it would certainly change the current structure. The parish priest should be part of the council but have no veto powers. This is changing the structure!!

In dioceses, a women should be appointed to senior posts including that of chancellor – as is already happening in some dioceses.

Number 9. Inclusive Liturgy

On the topic of women, the liturgy needs to be overhauled especially the Eucharistic prayers and readings, so that it is inclusive of men and women.

You Speak, We Listen

Q: Take the above points one by one and say whether you agree or disagree with them. Give your reasons.

Educational and attitudinal changes

Number 10. Sessions on "clericalism" in parish and diocese

What has happened to continuing adult faith development? (formerly "Adult Education in the Faith"?). Wilson's book is ideal for focusing on existing assumptions latent in clericalism and getting people to discuss them. Modern methods of education must be applied. The home rather than the parish centre could be tried as the venue because of its symbolism – always requiring parishioners to come to the church for events promotes clericalism.

Number 11. Examine our language

We can all trip up in our language and use words or expressions that betray clericalism. "We will have to ask Father". Perhaps we don't. Perhaps we simply need to inform him.

Every time we use the word "Father", we endorse the clericalism behind it. We want to say that this person is special and we hold him in honour. However, we can still respect a person and hold them in honour without using titles. At the weekly Eucharist, we do not introduce our friend as Professor Buongiorno, do we? We say, "This is John Buongiorno, or Bernice Clarke".

Some will still want to use "Father" and see its omission as lacking in respect. But respect is not something we can impose on others. Respect is earned. We should show respect to everyone in the church in the way we treat them, and they in return should treat us with respect.

Jean-Pierre Roche tells us this about his struggle with being called "father". His story is quite long but worth it.

> The Christians with whom I work and those I guide call me naturally by my first name, my baptismal name. However, all the Catholics I meet on Sundays, in the different churches in my community, or during baptisms, marriages and funerals, call me "Father". This is also true of the townspeople, who are not particularly Christian but who feel obliged to address me in this way.
>
> This has bothered me during the almost twenty years that I have been a priest. However, in today's context when we know that certain priests have been found guilty of the sexual abuse of children or nuns, I believe it is urgent that I ask of you: Please, do not call me "Father"!

He then gives us his three reasons why he does not want to be called "father". The first is based on the gospels, the second on avoiding infantilisation, and the third avoiding a false sense of obedience.

> The first reason should be sufficient in itself, as it is found in the Gospels. Priests wish to be disciples of Jesus, who said, "You are not to be called 'Master' for you have but one Master, and you are all brothers and sisters. And do not call anyone on earth 'Father'

for you have but one Father, who is in Heaven" (Matthew 23:8-9).

Sometimes Jesus' words are difficult to interpret, but the meaning of these is particularly clear. To be called "Father" is, quite frankly, to usurp the place of God, the Father of all people. It is, literally, to play God!

The second reason is that calling priests "Father" infantilises Catholics. How is it possible to have fraternal relationships between adults who are equals, if we are all brothers and sisters except for one person – the one we call "Father"? How do we dare express disagreement if, in doing so, we must "kill the father"?

Catholics are not children who have to say "Amen" each time the priest has spoken. The following is somewhat lengthy but some good points are made.

If the Church wants to once again be a fraternity, we must stop this custom, and should put into practice the beautiful passage from the Vatican Council II: "Even though some, by the will of Christ, are made doctors and pastors for the good of others, in terms of the dignity and activities of all the faithful in the edification of the Body of Christ, there is true equality among all."

I understand that priests exercise a sort of spiritual fatherhood. But I can say that those who see me as their spiritual guide never call me "Father".

So, is it to somehow compensate for not having children that priests let themselves be called "Father"?

What helps me to live my celibacy is that the fact that my mission has given me many friends. They are not children, but rather brothers and sisters. Isn't this what priests call us when they say, "Dear brothers and sisters"?

As for my brothers who are bishops (for whom I am saying many prayers at present), I leave it to them to ask you to no longer call them "Monsignor" or "My Lord". I find this particularly shocking, as we have only one "Signor"/"Lord". And it's not our bishop.

Finally, the practice of calling us "Father" can, quite frankly, be unhealthy when it is the expression of an emotional dependence based on a false idea of obedience.

Fatherhood is, in effect, a mixture of affection and authority. But it can be dangerous, especially if it is made sacred.[81]

You Speak, We Listen

Q: Take Jean-Pierre's three reasons for not wanting to be called "Father" and say why you agree or disagree with him.

Q: Why are some people in your parish called by their first name and others more formally?

---

81 Jean-Pierre Roche, "Stop calling me "Father"!, *La Croix International*, 13 August 2019, accessed on 5 November 2019.

Number 12. Give feedback honestly and non-abrasively

This is delicate. On the one hand we want to give honest and frank feedback; on the other hand, we don't want the receiver of the negative feedback to be so offended that they reject all the feedback in self-defence. A good approach is to try to balance positive and negative feedback. There is a tendency to only give negative feedback and one may ask where the origins of this tendency are located?

If no feedback is ever given, no change is likely. More than that, the offenders will presume that everything is okay. Sometimes timid people refrain from giving feedback because they do not want to offend anyone. But in doing so they reinforce the clericalism we are trying to eradicate. Sometimes when they give feedback, they are attacked.

Number 13. Explain servant role as in Vatican II and Pope Francis

This is what some call the God-talk or theology of service. One has only to go back to the gospels to find out. The disciples are called to be servants, not princes or lords over their people. Parish leaders must be creative in how this is done.

Number 14. Explain church as a community of equals rather than always a hierarchy

Stress what we have in common as parishioners: we want unity in our community; we want the opportunity to celebrate the Eucharist at least once a week; we want to use our gifts in the community ; we would like to see many ministries that serve the community. For us, this needs people to come forward. If they don't we won't have the ministries. If people do come forward, they want to be treated as adults (no infantilisation of the laity), and feel that their contributions are appreciated (an area often neglected). Thanking people publicly for their work and using incorrect names only exacerbates the hurt.

On the question of the church as a community of equals, one excellent lesson I witnessed was some years ago when our parish pastor left the sanctuary and sat in the first pew to listen to the readings at Mass. This showed us he was one of us.

Number 15. The meaning of Baptism

An ongoing explanation of Baptism and what the commitment requires; and the universal call to holiness.

Number 16. More time on "mission" and less on "maintenance"

Going beyond the inner circle in a parish to focus on the poor, marginalised and sick, can help a parish move from being priest-centred and dominated to other-centred; and thus help overcome clericalism.

Number 17. Avoid controlling or manipulating others

People should resist any attempts by whomever in the parish (ordained or lay) at "controlling" or "manipulating" others as has been done in the past. This will be a danger to lay persons as they step forward to contribute.

An authoritarian manner attempts to control people and not let them think for themselves or take initiatives. The times have changed and the individual now should do their own thinking and be guided by their conscience. The church has not always been the first to appreciate the need to shift from feudal dependency to taking personal responsibility. There must be a system of checks and balances so that there are no dictators.

> Clericalism, however, is the mindset not only of those whose leadership diminishes people's scope for exercising personal responsibility. It is also the mindset of those who prefer to be led in that way. Mere conformity to authority and to the law can be a cop-out for those who don't want to take personal responsibility. They prefer others to do the thinking and deciding. Those who still hanker for those times will certainly have difficulty with Pope Francis' style of leadership.[82]

Number 18. The I-God Relationship

The aim of the Christian life is about coming to the Father through Jesus in the Holy Spirit. It is about our relationship with our God. The bishop, priest or deacon, parish council chair, are simply a means to attain this goal, but not the only means.

(The word "priest" can be used as a verb, "to priest", meaning that every Christian tries to be a bridge between the human and divine. In encountering you, a person should be led to the divine. However, in the current situation, I think a change to using "pastor" would help people see the change required in the role.)

---

[82] Cullinane, op. cit.

You Speak, We Listen

Q: Now it is up to you. What concrete steps can you take either individually or in a group, to eradicate clericalism? Explain these steps to others in the group.

Appendix

A gospel roadmap to avoid clericalism

Leadership with service.

"You know that among the pagans the rulers lord it over them, and their great men make their authority felt. This is not to happen among you."

"Anyone who wants to be great among you must be your servant, and anyone who wants to be first among you must be your slave " (Matthew 20:27-28)

As many writers have pointed out, Jesus called forth disciples not from those high up in society at that time but from ordinary men and women. But no sooner had he called them out than the disciples were wondering about their status and who would be at Jesus' right hand.

"If anyone want to be first, he must make himself last of all and servant of all" (Mark 9:35-36)

"So always treat others as you would have them treat you; that is the meaning of the Law and the prophets" (Matthew 7:12)

"You must call no one on earth your father, since you have only one Father, and he is in heaven" (Matthew 23:9)

Jesus criticises the Scribes and Pharisees for hypocrisy and vanity.

"Everything they do is done to attract attention, like wearing broader phylacteries and longer tassels, like wanting to take the place of honour at banquets and the front seats in the synagogues, being greeted obsequiously in the market squares and having people call them Rabbi." (Matthew 23:5-7)